Praise for
All We Know of Pleasure

"I absolutely loved these poems and devoured them in one night—like a lover who wants to take her time but can't. They reminded me of what I first learned stealing Erica Jong off my mom's shelf when I was a teenager: sex is the force that drives the world, and women writing about it, with all that energy, particularity, sensuality, and humor, is the powerful force that cracks the world open."

—Jenna Blum, *New York Times* bestselling author of
Those Who Save Us and *The Lost Family*

All We Know of Pleasure: Poetic Erotica by Women is a breathtaking, eros driven, somatic poetic love letter to women's bodies. So many of the poets who changed my life and writing live inside this book, and isn't that the truth of it, that poets give our desires and ecstasies back to us? I read it with my whole body, dripping with delight.

—Lidia Yuknavitch, author of *The Book of Joan*
and *The Misfit's Manifesto*

T0125307

ALL WE KNOW OF PLEASURE

All
We Know
of
Pleasure

POETIC EROTICA BY WOMEN

Edited and with an Introduction
by Enid Shomer

BLAIR

Printed in South Korea
Cover design by Laura Williams
Interior Design by April Leidig
Typeset in Garamond Premier Pro and Matrix Inline Script
by Copperline Book Services, Inc.

Carolina Wren Press is a division of Blair.

*The mission of Carolina Wren Press is to seek out, nurture, and promote
literary work by new and underrepresented writers.*

We gratefully acknowledge the ongoing support of general operations
by the Durham Arts Council's United Arts Fund.

Library of Congress Control Number: 2018951880

Again, for L. T.

Contents

PART II
THE ORDINARY DAY BEGINS

PART III
WHEN THIS OLD BODY

Introduction

WHEN I WAS GROWING UP in the 1960s, there was a dearth of erotic reading material—the "dirty stuff" that all of us, boys and girls alike, eagerly sought. A dog-eared copy of Leon Uris's *Battle Cry* was furtively passed up and down the rows of my seventh-grade homeroom class with the "good parts" underlined. Later, we discovered entire books that were steamy—*Lady Chatterley's Lover* prime among them. At an age when we were innocent yet starved for information, such a book was a treasure trove, though it often confused and sometimes even frightened us. Would someone lace flowers in our pubic hair?

None of what we read was poetry, and none of it was written by women.

Nearly a century ago, Virginia Woolf explained to a skeptic that the reason there were so few good women writers was precisely the same reason there were so few *bad* women writers: that is, there were so few women writers at all. Thanks to the sexual revolution and the women's movement, the floodgates have been flung open, making available a rising tide of erotic literature. These women's voices are insistent, determined to share the experience of what it is like to live in a woman's body. Whether driven by love or lust or both, the poems in this anthology affirm womanhood at the most visceral level, unburdened by shame. They don't just describe the erotic; they re-enact it, capturing in words the variety and idiosyncrasy of sex.

While grief and mourning have the elegy, praise the ode, and seduction the sonnet, there is no established prosodic tradition for the erotic poem, no accepted formal vessel in which to pour passion to give it a familiar poetic shape. As a result, these poems experiment with form as well as content, displaying a pioneering spirit in their freshness, candor, humor, and inventiveness.

That august authority *The Princeton Encyclopedia of Poetry and Poetics* defines erotic poetry as "poetry which deals with the sexual in more or less explicit detail." It is "distinct on the one hand from love poetry, which traditionally avoids specifically sexual details . . . and on the other from mere pornographic . . . or obscene verse, which does not meet the aesthetic criteria . . . implied by the term poetry" (250).

I believe this anthology will broaden its readers' notions of what is erotic, for a glancing sample will demonstrate that the erotic permeates even the most mundane aspects of life, from reading a book to buying clothes. Concomitantly, the collection affirms the enormous meaningfulness of poetry, its ability to express the ineffable and to illuminate the most private and intimate of human experiences.

The poets here represent different ethnicities, geographies, social classes, and sexual orientations. The only characteristic they share is that they are women writing about sex.

The book is loosely organized along thematic lines. The poems in the first section focus on puberty, sexual initiation, and later experimentation as well. Some address subjects rarely spoken of before. For example, Marie Howe's "Practicing" details preteen girls kissing and feeling each other up in preparation for the men who will soon enter their lives. "Now you be the boy," they whisper, taking turns making each other moan. The suction noises of sex "horrify and thrill" the seventeen-year-old Elizabeth Alexander, without whose delightful poem they might otherwise go unremarked ("At Seventeen"). And what could be blunter and more powerful than Sharon Olds's acknowledgment that as a teenager "the cock / in our mouth, ah the cock in our mouth" was an outright surrogate for her father's? ("The Sisters of Sexual Treasure").

Adolescence brims with presentiments of the mystery that is sexuality. In "Fast Gas" Dorianne Laux envisions a "man waiting patiently / in my future like a red leaf / on the side-walk," someone, as Alice Fulton tells it, who will know how to "swindle the black heart / between my thighs" ("My Diamond Stud").

A recurring theme throughout this book is the equation of sex with language. "Tonight / we cross into each other's language," Olga Broumas announces in a poem about sex with a beloved ("Four Beginnings / for Kyra"). The speaker in "China" takes cocks into her mouth "like a warm vowel" (Laux). "I've read / the first draft of your body," Barbara Goldberg declares, as if her lover were a term paper in progress ("Foreshadows"). In Molly Peacock's poem about masturbation, language itself dissolves during orgasm. She can only mutter two phrases, both lacking syntax and grammar: "This is world-love. This is lost I'm" ("She Lays").

The second section probes the tension between extraordinariness and dailiness, between the excitement of the one-off and the stable satisfactions of regular sex with the same partner. What happens to the sizzling bedroom romp when a couple settles in for the long haul, with a mortgage and children and demanding jobs?

In the title poem of this section a woman watches her computer screen blink on, still feeling "the throb / of your last morning thrusts . . . echo" inside her (Saraceno, "The Ordinary Day Begins"). Sex is vital; it awakens "a hum . . . the sound something numb come alive makes" (Peacock, "The Purr").

Routine or exceptional, from the candlelit "careful screw" to the "grudge fuck, / the quick poke, / the hard core" (Videlock, "What Humans Do"), sex is transformative, putting us in touch with our primitive selves: "Anima, animus, we / descend into our evolutionary niche, / wild, demonic, from the bliss of it" (Goldberg, "Capitulation"). Sex triggers profound bodily knowledge, including an intimation of the body's demise: "Someday I'd like to die this way / with you still inside me" (Lee, "Seamless Beauty").

On other occasions, sex is merely companionable, "as if we'd / accomplished something together, / like climbing a hill or painting a house" (Laux, "Afterwards").

This section also recounts the ways the sexual urge descends upon us. One poet in a restaurant wants "To do it now. / To reach across the bread. / To start unbuttoning" (Clarke, "Buttons"). Conversely, the setting may be dully domestic, shaped by the cold realization that "When we fuck, stars don't peer down." Instead, "we lick and tickle each other" in "full view of the shower / head and bookcases" (Gerstler, "Housebound").

Many women write about their fascination with the penis, especially its ability "to grow and grow be- / tween my legs like a plant in fast motion" (Olds, "I Love It When"), to "rise like / bread baking, like / a helium balloon . . . like / an expandable drinking glass" (Bass, "In Celebration").

Female genitalia are equally enthralling, meriting description and praise. Audre Lorde finds "between your thighs the sweet / sharp taste of limes" ("On a night of the full moon"). Adrienne Rich refers to a "rose-wet cave" ("The Floating Poem, Unnumbered"). Olga Broumas proclaims that "Everything live / (tongue, clitoris, lip and lip) / swells in its moist shell" ("Amazon Twins"). In a humorous comparison of male and female, Ellen Bass cherishes "the puffy lips" of her partner's vulva but admits that "sometimes, I do miss a penis, / that nice thick flesh that hardens . . . I miss / feeling it nudge me from behind in the night, / poking in between my legs . . . [how] It jumps up in greeting like a setter" ("The Sad Truth").

In the third section we see the elegance of the body during sex, how men "lower their beautiful heads like horses drinking from a river / and taste me" (Addonizio, "Kisses"). Bodies are compared to "dolphins arcing like a wheel . . . stately giraffes . . . tigers stalking our sweet / prey" (Piercy, "The animal kingdom"). One's sexual history is a palimpsest, each act coloring and enriching the prior ones: "Every kiss is here somewhere, all over me like a fine, shiny / grit" (Addonizio, "Kisses").

Fantasies abound, often on a gargantuan scale. Hips, breasts, and vaginas become mountains, rivers, caves, clouds, and skies—sex and beauty of geological proportions. "There's a berth in my hips / as wide as the moon, / a ribcage roomier than the sea," Diane Ackerman boasts ("Song of the Current at Cape Horn"). Lucille Clifton brags "these hips are big hips . . . these hips are mighty hips . . . i have known them / to put a spell on a man and / spin him like a top!" ("homage to my hips").

Aging is another preoccupation here. The couple reunited at the airport in "Gate C22" is middle-aged and pudgy, but they kiss so passionately, so sweetly, that "We couldn't look away. We could / taste the kisses crushed in our mouths," the man gazing at the woman as if she were "the first sunrise seen from the Earth" (Bass). As the sexual response sharpens with time and experience "the sound / of a zipper can make you want to lie down / right where you are—" (Riegel, "To Endings").

Sex is a restorative that keeps at bay unpaid bills and accumulating emails, and, ultimately, "the wolf, the mongering wolf / who stands outside the self" (Kumin, "After Love"). During illness, too, desire can be a remedy of sorts, as in Ruth

Schwartz's poignant lines: "How savagely I want you, even here, / on the white stretcher, in the pallid hospital" ("January Vineyards"). And what could be more tender than the description of senior sex in Grace Paley's untitled poem which begins, "When this old body / finds that old body / what a nice day it is"?

There is more thematic variety—phone sex, food and sex, travel sex, and adultery—than there is room to itemize in this brief introduction. But no matter what the topic, all these poems make vivid the intimacy they describe. Many laud the splendor of mutuality, the generosity of the sex act between a loving pair. As Katherine Riegel opines, it is "—miraculous / as gravity—what he wants / is to give to me / and give to me / and give to me" ("Directions").

Life is brief and art is elegiac. After an intense experience—birth, death, sex, national tragedy—we have always reached for poetry as a way to celebrate or otherwise mark the event. To solemnify it.

My sincere hope is that these poems distill the pleasure and wonder their authors enjoyed in the flesh and that they prove a monument to the primal power of sex, that gift we all inherit.

—Enid Shomer
Tampa, Florida

PART I

The Discovery of Sex

Woman Reading

KATHLEEN FLENNIKEN

She licks her finger, little flick
of tongue and fingertip on furlough
to turn a page—

a motion that distracts her.
The thread of phrase   is broken
but for the word at turning—

vessel.
Vessel as in *ship* or *blood*?
She has to pause, all context lost

but blouse and skirt, this urge
to take them off

                           an ache

for something to contain it all.
Maybe *vessel*, maybe *"el"* alone,
bobbing on the tongue. Maybe

luscious, maybe just a finger to her lips
is all the afternoon
was asking for.

And lays aside her book.

In Ecstasy

ERIN BELIEU

at the altarpiece of Saint Teresa

No need to be coy—
you know what
she's doing.

And so did Bernini,
when he found Teresa
in the full-throttle of
her divine vision,
        caught her at it,

carving this surrender
so fluidly you expect
the impossible:

for her tang to swell up, ripe
as seafoam, from the gulf
of her flushed and falling
figure. Perhaps this is how

God comes to us,
or should come to us, all:

the bluntly and
beautifully corporeal at

prayers in the Sunday
school of pleasure. Why

shouldn't He come to us
as He did to Teresa? A saint

on her back—
a girl tearing open
the gift He gave her?

She Lays

MOLLY PEACOCK

She lays each beautifully mooned index finger
in the furrow on the right and on the left
sides of her clitoris and lets them linger
in their swollen cribs until the wish to see the shaft
exposed lets her move her fingers at the same time
to the right and left sides pinning back
the labia in a nest of hair, the pink sack
of folds exposed, the purplish ridge she'll climb,
when she lets one hand re-pin the labia
to free the other to wander with a withheld
purpose as if it were lost in the sands when the Via
To The City appeared suddenly, exposed:
when the whole exhausted mons is finally held
by both hands is when the Via gates are closed,

but they are open now, as open as her
thighs lying open among the arranged pillows.
Secrets have no place in the orchid boat of her
body and old pink brain beneath the willows.
This is self-love, assured, and this is lost time.
This is knowing, knowing, known
since growing, growing, grown;
revelation without astonishment,
understanding what is meant.
This is world-love. This is lost I'm.

Practicing

MARIE HOWE

I want to write a love poem for the girls I kissed in seventh
    grade,
a song for what we did on the floor in the basement

of somebody's parents' house, a hymn for what we didn't say
    but thought:
That feels good or *I like that*, when we learned how to open
    each other's mouths

how to move our tongues to make somebody moan. We
    called it practicing, and
one was the boy, and we paired off—maybe six or eight
    girls—and turned out

the lights and kissed and kissed until we were stoned on
    kisses, and lifted our
nightgowns or let the straps drop, and, Now you be the boy:

concrete floor, sleeping bag or couch, playroom, game room,
    train room, laundry.
Linda's basement was like a boat with booths and portholes

instead of windows. Gloria's father had a bar downstairs with
    stools that spun,
plush carpeting. We kissed each other's throats.

We sucked each other's breasts, and we left marks, and never
    spoke of it upstairs
outdoors, in daylight, not once. We did it, and it was

practicing, and slept, sprawled so our legs still locked or
    crossed, a hand still lost
in someone's hair . . . and we grew up and hardly mentioned
    who

the first kiss really was—a girl like us, still sticky with
    moisturizer we'd
shared in the bathroom. I want to write a song

for that thick silence in the dark, and the first pure thrill of
    unreluctant desire,
just before we made ourselves stop.

Corinna, Deplaning in Pittsburgh, Looks for Tessera, Her Friend from Summer Camp

STEPHANIE BURT

"Do I want to be with her? Or do I want to be her?"
The person I want or always wanted to be
is already on her way,
with all my half-expected, long-delayed
physicality,
the ropy muscles, the ribs you can touch, and
flowers. Cones of flowers. Nearly uncountable,
multiplied, uncrumpled-wrapping-paper
flowers, rosemary and baby's breath and a central array
of roses, like the center or the bud
we could feel together through cotton, through the
    uncountable, tiny
mechanically printed flowers
on the wireless (as in telegraph), underwireless bra
of the first girl I . . . the only girl I . . .

Either the rest of the world
is camp, with bunk beds and splinters and firewood
and challenging, never-silent mattresses,
or camp is the world, on the day we were all dismissed
to our cabins, given the pummeling rain,

the day we locked toes, and knees, and learned to believe
that we could actually exist.

It felt as if our very fingertips
had always been touching, as if the nervous connection
between us ran up our spines, and into our brains.

It was like lighting a match,
the only match in the whole world,
and being able to see
a face that could see me, all the way
through the as-if-predawn, lakeshore-foam-moss-colored
    mist.

And there she will be, across the jetway.

Is there any way to expect,
or just to be able to say,
that the anticipation is as exciting
as anything I can imagine we might
really do, tonight or today?

At Seventeen

ELIZABETH ALEXANDER

I want to do it, want to snort and root
and forage in your skin and apertures.
It happens fast. It hits a frantic pitch.

I want to touch touch, suck suck, lick lick
like my kin in the animal kingdom.
Suction noises horrify and thrill me,

forensic evidence of what I'm doing
and doing and doing, pants around
my ankles, twigs in my hair. I am

sweaty and dirty, a little bit bloody,
smell of exactly what I have been
up to, sneak home like the criminal I am,

new memory like a seltzer in my crotch.

First Sex

SHARON OLDS

(For J.)

I knew little, and what I knew
I did not believe—they had lied to me
so many times, so I just took it as it
came, his naked body on the sheet,
the tiny hairs curling on his legs like
fine, gold shells, his sex
harder and harder under my palm
and yet not hard as a rock his face cocked
back as if in terror, the sweat
jumping out of his pores like sudden
trails from the tiny snails when his knees
locked with little clicks and under my
hand he gathered and shook and the actual
flood like milk came out of his body, I
saw it glow on his belly, all they had
said and more, I rubbed it into my
hands like lotion, I signed on for the duration.

Stairway to Heaven

JILL BIALOSKY

My girlfriend and I snuck out
of our houses at midnight
on a Cleveland winter night
and met at the corner of our block.
Our mission was to find the two gas station
attendants we had spotted the night before.
We didn't know their names,
only their oily hands and dark coats.
Marie had big boobs and soft, Chek lips.
I was a quiet teenager with slight curves
and deep, skirting eyes.
We were a sensible team:
she was the target and I was the protection.
One boy was cuter than the other,
that's how it always went.
Marie would get in the back seat
and neck with the cute one
and I'd stay in front pressed against
the passenger door talking to the gawky driver
with a scar underneath his eye or bad teeth
above the sound of "Stairway to Heaven" or something
by Fleetwood Mac, until their lips in the back
were bruised and puffy.
Eventually, the driver pulled over
and let us out at the curb.
Marie scribbled her phone number on a matchbook.
For two or three days we'd linger near the phone
until pissed-off and pumped with revenge
we'd go out again, stalking the night

for the new replacements.
This time was my turn, I decided.
Outside the Sohio
we leaned against the unleaded
and waited for their shift to end.
When we got to the car
I slipped in the back,
ignoring Marie's tug on my sleeve.
The good one slipped in next.
The tape began: "Lucy in the Sky with Diamonds,"
joint lit, and within minutes
we were in the haze of music and drug
until we'd open the door
and let the cold blast of air rescue us.
His name was Randy.
The very minute the words slipped
from his lips I didn't want to forget him.
Randy, I thought, over and over
as he turned a lock of my hair
in his finger and began his work.
No, I *liked* the smell of petroleum
on his neck, his nicotine lips.
I could make him up in my mind
for weeks, I thought, without
knowing a single thing about him.
This time we'd wait by my phone
and when it rang I'd say, Randy,
Hello. Two words.
And the long dark dialogue
would begin.

The Sisters of Sexual Treasure

SHARON OLDS

As soon as my sister and I got out of our
mother's house, all we wanted to
do was fuck, obliterate
her tiny sparrow body and narrow
grasshopper legs. The men's bodies
were like our father's body! The massive
hocks, flanks, thighs, elegant
knees, long tapered calves—
we could have him there, the steep forbidden
buttocks, backs of the knees, the cock
in our mouth, ah the cock in our mouth.
                    Like explorers who
discover a lost city, we went
nuts with joy, undressed the men
slowly and carefully, as if
uncovering buried artifacts that
proved our theory of the lost culture:
that if Mother said it wasn't there,
it was there.

Bar Napkin Sonnet #11

MOIRA EGAN

Things happen when you drink too much mescal.
One night, with not enough food in my belly,
he kept on buying.   I'm a girl who'll fall
damn near in love with gratitude and, well, he
was hot and generous and so the least
that I could do was let him kiss me, hard
and soft and any way you want it, beast
and beauty, lime and salt—sweet Bacchus' pards—
and when his friend showed up I felt so warm
and generous I let him kiss me too.
His buddy asked me if it was the worm
inside that makes me do the things I do.
I wasn't sure which worm he meant, the one
I ate?   The one that eats at me alone?

Have You Ever Faked an Orgasm?

MOLLY PEACOCK

When I get nervous, it's so hard not to.
When I'm expected to come in something
other than my ordinary way, to
take pleasure in the new way, lost, not knowing

how to drive it back to sureness . . . where are
the thousand thousand flowers I always pass,
the violet flannel, then the sharpness?
I can't, I can't . . . extinguish the star

in a burst. It goes on glowing. Your head
between my legs so long. Do you really
want to be there? I whimper as though . . .
then get mad. I could smash your valiant head.

"You didn't come, did you?" Naturally, you know.
Although I try to lie, the truth escapes me
almost like an orgasm itself. Then the "No"
that should crack a world, but doesn't, slips free.

Fast Gas

DORIANNE LAUX

for Richard

Before the days of self service,
when you never had to pump your own gas,
I was the one who did it for you, the girl
who stepped out at the sound of a bell
with a blue rag in my hand, my hair pulled back
in a straight, unlovely ponytail.
This was before automatic shut-offs
and vapor seals, and once, while filling a tank,
I hit a bubble of trapped air and the gas
backed up, came arcing out of the hole
in a bright gold wave and soaked me—face, breasts,
belly and legs. And I had to hurry
back to the booth, the small employee bathroom
with the broken lock, to change my uniform,
peel the gas-soaked cloth from my skin
and wash myself in the sink.
Light-headed, scrubbed raw, I felt
pure and amazed—the way the amber gas
glazed my flesh, the searing,
subterranean pain of it, how my skin
shimmered and ached, glowed
like rainbowed oil on the pavement.
I was twenty. In a few weeks I would fall,
for the first time, in love, that man waiting
patiently in my future like a red leaf
on the sidewalk, the kind of beauty
that asks to be noticed. How was I to know

it would begin this way: every cell of my body
burning with a dangerous beauty, the air around me
a nimbus of light that would carry me
through the days, how when he found me,
weeks later, he would find me like that,
an ordinary woman who could rise
in flame, all he would have to do
is come close and touch me.

My Diamond Stud

ALICE FULTON

He'll be a former cat burglar
because I have baubles
to lose. I'll know him
by the black
carnation he's tossing:
heads, he takes me,
stems, the same. Yes,
he'll be a hitchhiker at this
roller-rink I frequent, my diamond
stud who'll wheel up shedding
sparks & say "*Ecoutez
bé-bé.* I'm a member
of a famous folded trapeze
act. My agility is legend, etc."
keeping his jeweler's eye on
my gold fillings. He'll know
what I really want: whipping
me with flowers, his fingers' grosgrain
sanded smooth, raw
to my every move. For our tryst
we'll go to travel-folder heaven
& buff-puff each other's
calluses in valentine tubs.
He'll swindle the black heart
between my thighs
dress me up in Ultra-
suede sheaths, himself

in Naugahyde. No,
leather. He'd never
let anything touch him
that wasn't once alive.

The 4-Barrel Carburetor On a '72 Chevy Camaro

LORNA DEE CERVANTES

He could make love like a 4-barrel
carburetor on a '72 Chevy
Camaro. Man, he could go. Pumping up
the pistons, discharging with a growl.
He wasn't all that to look at, mostly gleaming
chrome and wire. Slick in the upholstery
and revved. He was a 2-bucket seat
palace, a chariot of wiles. He was
coming back. He was a place off the map.
He was coming home and he was moving.
He was a reserved parking space, a handicapped
spot on the heart. He was a ticket
waiting to be written, a stop-on-a-
dime promise of forgiveness. He could
pick up in the alley, carry away on the charm
of his engine. All the draft on a knife
point of design and desire, his get up
and go: his knack.

"What Do Women Want?"

KIM ADDONIZIO

I want a red dress.
I want it flimsy and cheap,
I want it too tight, I want to wear it
until someone tears it off me.
I want it sleeveless and backless,
this dress, so no one has to guess
what's underneath. I want to walk down
the street past Thrifty's and the hardware store
with all those keys glittering in the window,
past Mr. and Mrs. Wong selling day-old
donuts in their café, past the Guerra brothers
slinging pigs from the truck and onto the dolly,
hoisting the slick snouts over their shoulders.
I want to walk like I'm the only
woman on earth and I can have my pick.
I want that red dress bad.
I want it to confirm
your worst fears about me,
to show you how little I care about you
or anything except what
I want. When I find it, I'll pull that garment
from its hanger like I'm choosing a body
to carry me into this world, through
the birth-cries and the love-cries too,
and I'll wear it like bones, like skin,
it'll be the goddamned
dress they bury me in.

Navy

BARBARA O'DAIR

He jackknifed me over the bathtub faucet,

Fucked me four times that morning,

Fat and beating, like a fish.

Furious, slippery, typical,

We won the war on water

Again and again and again.

Otherwise, we met at Pacific docksides,

He and I over the undertow.

I would end up wrapped around a margarita.

And my stepmother said I was a whore.

So be it, I replied.

The fleet is in.

Preference

BETH GYLYS

Some people need a harsher kind of love.
I like the smooth soft wetness of our sex.
I like the gentle easy way we move,

our bodies blending in a fleshy weave,
our lips, torsos, tongues a sensuous mix.
Some people need a harsher kind of love.

One plays the master, the other plays the slave.
They plunge each other's depths with plastic dicks.
I like him gentle. I like his easy move

against me, desire rising like a wave
that draws us slowly to its crest then breaks.
Some women need a harsher kind of love.

A brutish forceful man is what they crave.
They scream and bite; they claw their lovers' backs.
I like the gentle, easy way you move,

and taste and touch my skin, without a glove,
or ropes to bind me. How could I relax,
confronted with a harsher kind of love?
I'll take the gentle, easy way we move.

Your Shower

NIKKI GIOVANNI

I wish I could be
Your shower
I would bubble
Your hair
Tickle my way
Down to your lips
Across your shoulders
And over your back
Around your waist
Bouncing off your knees
Fall to the tips
Of your toes
Then journey back
Again
Warm   Wet
Sticky   Sweet
Up and Down
Around and Around
Around and Around
Around and Around
Until
There is
No more hot
Water

Your Hands

ANGELINA WELD GRIMKÉ

       I love your hands:
They are big hands, firm hands, gentle hands;
Hair grows on the back near the wrist . . . .
I have seen the nails broken and stained
From hard work.
And yet, when you touch me,
I grow small . . . . and quiet . . . . . .
. . . . And happy . . . .
If I might only grow small enough
To curl up into the hollow of your palm,
Your left palm,
Curl up, lie close and cling,
So that I might know myself always there,
. . . . Even if you forgot.

Fishing Seahorse Reef

ENID SHOMER

Our lures trail
in the prop-wash,
skipping to mimic
live bait. Minutes ago
I watched you
cut up the dead shrimp
that smell like sex.
Now we stand, long
filmy shapes jigsawed
by the waves, and wait
for the rods to arc
heavy with kingfish.
We bring the limit
of eight on board,
their teeth gnashing
against the lures.
And I think how tender
all animal urgency is—
these fish thrashing
to throw the hook,
or a man flinging himself
into the future
each time he enters
a woman. This
is what I picture
all afternoon: you
inside me, your body a stem
bent under the weight
of its flowering,

as beautiful as that;
how carefully
you would lower yourself,
like something winged,
a separate order
of fallen thing
from these angels with fins
who know only once
the difference
between water and air.

When Man Enters Woman

ANNE SEXTON

When man
enters woman,
like the surf biting the shore,
again and again,
and the woman opens her mouth in pleasure
and her teeth gleam
like the alphabet,
Logos appears milking a star,
and the man
inside of woman
ties a knot
so that they will
never again be separate
and the woman
climbs into a flower
and swallows its stem
and Logos appears
and unleashes their rivers.

This man,
this woman
with their double hunger,
have tried to reach through
the curtain of God
and briefly they have,
though God
in His perversity
unties the knot.

China

DORIANNE LAUX

From behind he looks like a man
I once loved, that hangdog slouch
to his jeans, a sweater vest, his neck
thick-veined as a horse cock, a halo
of chopped curls.

He orders coffee and searches
his pockets, first in front, then
from behind, a long finger sliding
into the slitted denim the way that man
slipped his thumb into me one summer
as we lay after love, our freckled
bodies two pale starfish on the sheets.

Semen leaked and pooled in his palm
as he moved his thumb slowly, not
to excite me, just to affirm
he'd been there.

I have loved other men since, taken
them into my mouth like a warm vowel,
lain beneath them and watched their irises
float like small worlds in their open eyes.

But this man pressed his thumb
toward the tail of my spine
as if he were entering
China, or a ripe papaya,
so that now
when I think of love
I think of this.

The Source

SHARON OLDS

It became the deep spring of my life,
I didn't know if it was a sickness or a gift.
To reach around both sides of a man,
one palm to one buttock,
the other palm to the other, the way we are split,
to grasp that band of muscle on the male
haunch and help guide the massed
heavy nerve down my throat until it
stoppers the hole behind the breastbone that is always
    hungry,
then I feel complete. To be lifted
onto a man — the male breast
so hard, there seem no chambers in it, it is
lifting-muscle — and set tight as a lock-slot down
onto a bolt, we are looking into
each other's eyes as if the matter of the iris were
a membrane deep in the body dissolving now,
it is what I had dreamed, to meet men
fully, as a woman twin, unborn,
half-gelled, clasped, nothing between us
but our bodies, naked, and when those dissolve,
nothing between us — or perhaps I vanish
and the man is still there, as if I have been trying
to disappear, into them,
to be myself the glass of sourmash
my father lifted to his mouth. Ah, I am in him,
I slide all the way down to the beginning, the
curved chamber of the balls. My brothers
and sisters are there, swimming by the cinerous

millions, I say to them, Stay here—
for the children of this father it may be the better life;
but they cannot hear. Blind, deaf,
armless, brainless, they plunge forward,
driven, desperate to enter the other, to
die in her, and wake. For a moment,
after we wake, we are without desire—
five, ten, twenty seconds of
pure calm, as if each one of us is whole.

The French Bed

IDRIS ANDERSON

I can't speak from the man's point of view,
but as a woman, I'd say this etching tells truth
about sex. The lover is kneeling for his own pleasure
first, then hers too, perhaps. His foot is flexed
for pushing energetically. He's as deep
as he can go into the soft folds of her flesh.
And she, with knees frankly spread, is telling him
with fingers where and how he should move.
Notice the eyes, they are so wise with each other.
It's not a brothel. He was in love with this wife.

Rembrandt, in his exuberance, gave the girl
three arms. One hand we see stroking the side
of her lover's back, another reaches round for his bum,
and the third, a fully visible limb, lies limp
on the bed, as if she's totally compliant, or done.
The bed is well made, with canopy and draperies,
the linens as plush as her thighs. She's relaxed into what
he desires; she's eager and wants her own pleasure too.
The drypoint's velvety strokes so accurate. He saw
what he wanted and made it, and wanted what he saw.

After all the crosses, Christs feeding the peasants,
rooftops and ruins, beggars in hats, here is
domestic interior—fine inked-up lines swirled
into rumpled bedclothes and bodies' vulnerable
curlings—her sweet face, his competent shoulders.
A scribbling style, tender and swift, all gesture

and touch. The needle's hard burr softens and makes
vivid the intimacy, the inwardness, the mutual desire.
What comes after seduction, the drapery drawn
for our eyes—what we want desperately is this.

Breasts

MAXINE CHERNOFF

If I were French, I'd write
about breasts, structuralist treatments
of breasts, deconstructionist breasts,
Gertrude Stein's breasts in Père Lachaise
under stately marble. Film noir breasts
no larger than olives, Edith Piaf's breasts
shadowed under a song, mad breasts raving
in the bird market on Sunday.
Tanguy breasts softening the landscape,
the politics of nipples (we're all equal).
A friend remembers nursing,
his twin a menacing blur. But wait,
we're in America, where breasts
were pointy until 1968. I once invented
a Busby Berkeley musical with naked women
underwater sitting at a counter
where David Bowie soda-jerked them
ice cream glaciers. It sounds so sexual
but had a Platonic airbrushed air.
Beckett calls them dugs, which makes me think
of potatoes, but who calls breasts potatoes?
Bolshoi dancers strap down their breasts
while practicing at the barre.
You guess they're thinking of sailing,
but probably it's bread, dinner,
and the *Igor Zlotik Show* (their
Phil Donahue). There's a photo of me
getting dressed where I'm surprised
by Paul and try to hide my breasts, and another

this year, posed on a pier, with my breasts
reflected in silver sunglasses. I blame
it on summer when flowers overcome gardens
and breasts point at the stars. Cats
have eight of them, and Colette tells
of a cat nursing its young while
being nursed by its mother. Imagine the scene
rendered human. And then there's the Russian
story about the woman . . . but wait,
they've turned the lights down, and Humphrey
Bogart is staring at Lauren Bacall's breasts
as if they might start speaking.

Wet

MARGE PIERCY

Desire urges us on deeper
and farther into the coral maze
of the body, dense, tropical
where we cannot tell plant
from animal, mind from body
prey from predator, swaying
magenta, teal, green-golden
anemones weaving wide open.

The stronger lusts flash
corn rows of dagger teeth,
but the little desires slip,
sleek frisky neon flowers
into the corners of the eye.
The mouth tastes their strange
sweet and salty blood
burning the back of the tongue.

Deeper and deeper into
the thick warm translucence
where mind and body melt,
where we see with our tongues
and taste with our fingers;
there the horizon of excess
folds as we approach
into plains of not enough.

Now we are returned to ourselves
flung out on the beach

exhausted, flanks heaving
out of oxygen and time,
grinning like childish daubs
of boats. Now it is sleep
draws us down, surrendered
to its dark glimmer.

Lullaby

MOLLY PEACOCK

Big as a down duvet the night
pulls the close Ontario sky
over the naked earth. Here we lie
gossiping in a circle of light

under our own big comforter,
buried nude as bulbs. I slide south
to grow your hyacinth in my mouth.
Far above, the constellations blur

on the comforter that real sky
is to real earth. Stars make a pattern
above; down here our pattern is fireflies
on flannel around us. Night turns

to surround the planet. Earth settles
real hyacinths in place. You yield,
turning like night's face to settle
on me, chest on breasts, your field.

Orion's Belt

BRENDA HILLMAN

Read this by your own light,
little body;
read this with your eyes closed;

under the three stars
you learned the origins of love.

When they took you out,
you would push the buttons of their jeans
with your thumb

and the stars stretched in Orion's belt
like the three mysteries
at the start of time.

Dentyne and dope
on their breath—mostly Dentyne.
Long warm breath

between watching spaces, between
the light that left Orion
a million years ago,   and they

tried to see no body
up there, no guilty party,

but to speak of the forces
that made them: hydrogen, helium,
like legendary women,

and at the edge of the universe,
a little buzzing—like a phone left off the hook . . .

They lay on the hoods of cars
(warm engine: ticking) and you
undid their belts;—

Orion lay on his right side,
then on his left, his belt
undone, the three stars

doomed to circle
like the three mysteries at the start of time:

why it happened,
why we suffer,
and how love bothers at all . . .

When you think of those
you will not touch again
in this lifetime

you own a few points on the one body.
Some made you happy.
Everything else—

the pale sword of the hunter,
the uplifted sandal,

everything else mostly fades
in the folds of heaven—

Attraction

ENID SHOMER

The whites of his eyes
pull me like moons.
He smiles. I believe
his face. Already
my body slips down in the chair:

I recline on my side,
offering peeled grapes.
I can taste his tongue
in my mouth
whenever he speaks.

I suspect he lies.
But my body oils itself loose.
When he gets up to fix a drink
my legs like derricks
hoist me off the seat.
I am thirsty, it seems.

Already I see the seduction
far off in the distance
like a large tree
dwarfed by a rise
in the road.

I put away objections
as quietly as quilts.
Already I explain to myself
how marriages are broken—
accidentally, like arms or legs.

Space Race

COLETTE LABOUFF ATKINSON

I knew him before he was broken. He wanted me and I wanted to break him. And then I wanted him not to want me anymore. And then I wanted him to call. When it happened—all of it in just that order—I drove to his house. We watched the longest movie, *The Right Stuff*, which I had the patience to sit through since I knew at the end we'd have sex. Somewhere in the film, in the middle of an argument about how chasing women who don't matter can ruin everything, Gus Grissom says *The issue here ain't pussy. The issue is monkey.* And that movie watching had nothing to do with space or history or men or monkeys. All he wanted was sex. I'd waited a couple of years for that: to have seen him broken and mended and then looking right through me, right on to the stars. I would still want to mean so little that I'd be see-thru. Sometimes I can daydream him back to breakable. Mostly, I would want to watch movies with him while he's in love with someone else and helping himself to me.

The Shyness

SHARON OLDS

Then, when we were joined, I became
shyer. I became completed, joyful,
and shyer. I may have shone more, reflected
more, and from deep inside there rose
some glow passing steadily through me, but I was not
playing, now, I felt like someone
small, in a raftered church, or in
a cathedral, the vaulted spaces of the body
like a sacred woods. I was quiet when my throat was not
making those iron, orbital, rusted,
coming noises at the hinge of matter and
whatever is not matter. He takes me into
ending after ending like another world at the
center of this one, and then, if he begins to
end when I am resting I feel awe, I almost feel
fear, sometimes for a moment I feel
I should not move, or make a sound, as
if he is alone, now,
howling in the wilderness,
and yet I know we are in this place
together. I thought, now is the moment
I could become more loving, and my hands moved shyly
over him, secret as heaven,
and my mouth spoke, and in my beloved's
voice, by the bones of my head, the fields
groaned, and then I joined him again,
not shy, not bold, released, entering
the true home, where the trees bend down along the
ground and yet stand, then we lay together

panting, as if saved from some disaster, and for ceaseless
instants, it came to pass what I have
heard about, it came to me
that I did not know I was separate
from this man, I did not know I was lonely.

Desire

DEIDRE POPE

clit
      breasts
lips   legs   luscious
                                       ass

separating the parts is not a feminist thing to do

curve of ankle
fingertips

but the way you look in jeans
is not the way you look in nothing
but my shirt

        and the way I breathe
        when you flick my nipple with your tongue
        is not the way I breathe
        when your hand is inside
        me like a nested bird

cunt   throat   middle finger   breast-bone

if one thing leads to another
then I begin with your hair
your eyes   followed by
your mouth
long neck
and there I'm unbuttoning your shirt
and will itemize

every inch of you
with my hot tongue greedy fingers my
whole body (which is nothing
other than its parts) calculating the sum
of yours

Skylight

JAYNE RELAFORD BROWN

Lie here, you say.
The clouds are sailing by.
The wind's picked up.

Careful not to touch, I stretch
along your body, place my head
a fraction of an inch from yours

inside the small square
of light-charged air
that heats your comforter.

Look up, you murmur,
See the way they slide?
I watch, grow dizzy with the pace

as white silks slip across
the turquoise frame, as your cool breath
moves moist against my ear.

This is where I love
to lie and dream, you say. And here's
The moment I could tell you

I've been dreaming too, of you,
or simply turn my face
and meet your lips,

the moment I could trust
I understand your hints,

and why you've brought me
to this place.

And if I kissed you
softly as a cloud,
traveled over you
as slowly as a mist,

and entered you
as gentle as a fog,
would I be
as welcome as a rain?

Would you lie still,
watch sky as if I
wasn't touching you?
Would you run?

Or would you sigh,
so glad to have
the waiting done,
and turn to me,

and could we two,
together, gather
like a storm?

Black Slip

TERRY WOLVERTON

She told me she had always fantasized
about a woman in a black slip.
It had to do with Elizabeth Taylor
in *Butterfield Eight*.

She came to my house with a huge box
gift-wrapped with gigantic ribbons.
Inside, a black slip.

Slinky, with lace across the bodice.
She told me how she was embarrassed
in the department store,
a woman in men's pants
buying a black slip clearly not intended for herself,
and about the gay men in line behind her,
sharing the joke.

She asked me to try it on.
I took it into the bathroom, slipped it over my head.
I stared at myself for a long time
before I came out of the bathroom
walked over to her
lying on the bed.

That was the first time. It got easier.
The black slip was joined by a blue slip
then a red one
then a long lavender negligee, the back slit to there.

I wore them to bed.
In the morning she would smile and say
how much she loved waking up next to a woman in a slip.
The black slip remained our favorite.
We always made love when I wore the black slip.

Once I showed up at her door late at night
wearing a long coat
with only the black slip underneath.

One night I cooked dinner at her apartment
wearing nothing but the black slip
and red suede high heels.

It was always the first thing to pack when we went on
        vacation.

And she used to make me promise
that if we ever broke up
I'd never wear that slip for anyone else.

I don't know where it is now.

Stripped of that private skin
when we broke up
I never went back to claim it.

I think she must have
packed it
given it
thrown it
away.

On bad days I imagine her
sliding it over the head of some new love
whispering about Elizabeth Taylor
and waking up to a woman in a slip.

Or perhaps
it's still there
draped on the back of the door.

A sinuous shadow.

A moan in the dark.

First Poem for You

KIM ADDONIZIO

I like to touch your tattoos in complete
darkness, when I can't see them. I'm sure of
where they are, know by heart the neat
lines of lightning pulsing just above
your nipple, can find, as if by instinct, the blue
swirls of water on your shoulder where a serpent
twists, facing a dragon. When I pull you

to me, taking you until we're spent
and quiet on the sheets, I love to kiss
the pictures in your skin. They'll last until
you're seared to ashes; whatever persists
or turns to pain between us, they will still
be there. Such permanence is terrifying.
So I touch them in the dark; but touch them, trying.

The Lovers

DORIANNE LAUX

She is about to come. This time,
they are sitting up, joined below the belly,
feet cupped like sleek hands praying
at the base of each other's spines.
And when something lifts within her
toward a light she's sure, once again,
she can't bear, she opens her eyes
and sees his face is turned away,
one arm behind him, hand splayed
palm down on the mattress, to brace himself
so he can lever his hips, touch
with the bright tip the innermost spot.
And she finds she *can't* bear it—
not his beautiful neck, stretched and corded,
not his hair fallen to one side like beach grass,
not the curved wing of his ear, washed thin
with daylight, deep pink of the inner body.
What she can't bear is that she can't see his face,
not that she thinks this exactly—she is rocking
and breathing—it's more her body's thought,
opening, as it is, into its own sheer truth.
So that when her hand lifts of its own volition
and slaps him, twice on the chest,
on that pad of muscled flesh just above the nipple,
slaps him twice, fast, like a nursing child
trying to get a mother's attention,
she's startled by the sound,
though when he turns his face to hers—
which is what her body wants, his eyes

pulled open, as if she had bitten—
she does reach out and bite him, on the shoulder,
not hard, but with the power infants have
over those who have borne them, tied as they are
to the body, and so, tied to the pleasure,
the exquisite pain of this world.
And when she lifts her face he sees
where she's gone, knows she can't speak,
is traveling toward something essential,
toward the core of her need, so he simply
watches, steadily, with an animal calm
as she arches and screams, watches the face that,
if she could see it, she would never let him see.

Directions

KATHERINE RIEGEL

After the kisses that swell my lips
and tongue, after the fingertips circling
my nipple like water
circling the drain, coming nearer
and nearer to the center, that sucking
sound, after the push
that sends my shoulders onto the bed
and my knees open to his hand,

I can still say *gentle* and his finger lifts,
touches light as a moth. His breath
is heavy and his teeth
graze my clavicle but he listens
with his whole body, he touches
soft until I am slick and then
he keeps touching soft because
that is what I want and—miraculous
as gravity—what he wants
is to give to me
and give to me
and give to me.

The Discovery of Sex

DEBRA SPENCER

We try to be discreet standing in the dark
hallway by the front door. He gets his hands
up inside the front of my shirt and I put mine
down inside the back of his jeans. We are crazy
for skin, each other's skin, warm silky skin.
Our tongues are in each other's mouths,
where they belong, home at last. At first

we hope my mother won't see us, but later we don't care,
we forget her. Suddenly she makes a noise
like a game show alarm and says *Hey! Stop that!*
and we put our hands out where she can see them.
Our mouths stay pressed together, though, and
when she isn't looking anymore our hands go
back inside each other's clothes. We could

go where no one can see us, but we are
good kids, from good families, trying to have
as much discreet sex as possible with my mother and father
four feet away watching strangers kiss on TV,
my mother and father who once did as we are doing,
something we can't imagine because we know

that before we put our mouths together, before
the back seat of his parents' car where our skins
finally become one—before us, these things
were unknown! Our parents look on in disbelief
as we pioneer delights they thought only they knew
before those delights gave them us.

Years later, still we try to be discreet, standing
in the kitchen now where we think she can't see us. I
slip my hands down inside the back of his jeans
and he gets up under the front of my shirt.
We open our mouths to kiss and suddenly *Hey! Hey!*
says our daughter glaring from the kitchen doorway.
Get a room! she says, as we put our hands
out where she can see them.

Desire

JANE HIRSHFIELD

For years, the habit of wanting you,
carried like something unnoticed,
lint in a pocket, or manzanita
seed waiting a fire—
you come to me
changed, an old photograph
blurred with motion,
the shutter too slow to keep you the same.
After a while, the light, an old habit
between us, drains off:
simple to meet, to walk towards evening
in a park at the continent's edge;
simple to talk
until conversation drains off,
a newly decanted wine,
and we're left with the sediment dark
at bottom between us,
desire,
simple to say,
and all the decision pours out of my life,
leaving me buoyant, empty, to float
towards your hand.

PART II

The
Ordinary Day
Begins

Kissing Again

DORIANNE LAUX

Kissing again, after a long drought of
not kissing—too many kids, bills, windows

needing repair. Sex, yes, though squeezed in
between the minor depths of anger, despair—

standing up amid the laundry
or fumbling onto the strip of rug between

the coffee table and the couch. Quick, furtive,
like birds. A dance on the wing, but no time

for kissing, the luxuriant tonguing of another
spongy tongue, the deft flicking and feral sucking,

that prolonged lapping that makes a smooth stone
of the brain. To be lost in it, your body tumbled

in sea waves, no up or down, just salt
and the liquid swells set in motion

by the moon, by a tremor in Istanbul, the waft
of a moth wing before it plows into a halo of light.

Praise the deep lustrous kiss that lasts minutes,
blossoms into what feels like days, fields of tulips

glossy with dew, low purple clouds piling in
beneath the distant arch of a bridge. One

after another they storm your lips, each kiss
a caress, autonomous and alive, spilling

into each other, streams into creeks into rivers
that grunt and break upon the gorge. Let the tongue,

in its wisdom, release its stores, let the mouth,
tired of talking, relax into its shapes of give

and receive, its plush swelling, its slick
round reveling, its primal reminiscence

that knows only the one robust world.

The Ordinary Day Begins

JUNE SYLVESTER SARACENO

at my desk
the screen blinks on
numbers begin their race
but inside me, the throb
of your last morning thrusts
continue, echo
you in me

the quiet seep of love spreads
I smile in secret
the computer hums
I, too, am humming, low
waves receding
washes of warm light

figures flit and flash
numbers, columns, rows,
I stare and suck my lower lip
that tastes of you,
your last kiss lingers
long after the ordinary day begins

The Knowing

SHARON OLDS

Afterwards, when we have slept, paradise-
comaed, and woken, we lie a long time
looking at each other.
I do not know what he sees, but I see
eyes of quiet evenness
and endurance, a patience like the dignity
of matter. I love the open ocean
blue-grey-green of his iris, I love
the curve of it against the white,
that curve the sight of what has caused me
to go over, when he's quite still, deep
inside me. I have never seen a curve
like that, except our sphere, from outer
space. I don't know where he got
his kindness without self-regard,
almost without self, and yet
he chose one woman, instead of the others.
By knowing him, I get to know
the purity of the animal
which mates for life. Sometimes he is slightly
smiling, but mostly he just gazes at me gazing,
his entire face lit. I love
to see it change if I cry—there is no worry,
no pity, a graver radiance. If we
are on our backs, side by side,
with our faces turned fully to face each other,
I can hear a tear from my lower eye
hit the sheet, as if it is an early day on earth,
and then the upper eye's tears

braid and sluice down through the lower eyebrow
like the invention of farming, irrigation, a non-nomadic
    people.
I am so lucky that I can know him.
This is the only way to know him.
I am the only one who knows him.
When I wake again, he is still looking at me,
as if he is eternal. For an hour
we wake and doze, and slowly I know
that though we are sated, though we are hardly
touching, this is the coming that the other
brought us to the edge of—we are entering,
deeper and deeper, gaze by gaze,
this place beyond the other places,
beyond the body itself, we are making
love.

The Purr

MOLLY PEACOCK

As you stand still in the hall thinking what
to do next and I approach you from behind,
I think behind must be best: your naked
rump scalloped beneath the plumb

line of your spine's furred tree. But
as I catch the concentration in the kind
angling of your head toward the cats and tread
catlike myself behind you, your scrotum

hung like an oriole's nest, I cut
beneath your outstretched arm and find
I'm hungry for your face instead,
hungry for my future. The mysterious thrum

that science can't yet explain awakes a hum
in me, the sound something numb come alive makes.

In the Kitchen

STACIE CASSARINO

It's right before you drive away:
our limbs still warm with sleep,
coffee sputtering out, the north
wind, your hips pressing me
hard against the table. I like it hard
because I need to remember this.
I want to say harder. How we must
look to the road that's gone,
to the splayed morning of cold
butter and inveterate greed.
Light comes and goes in the field.
Oranges in a bowl, garlic, radio.
In the story of us, no one wins.
Isolation is a new theme
someone says. By now
I've invented you. Most people
don't like to touch dead things.
That's what my friend tells me
when I find my fish on the floor.
It must have wanted an out.
Sometimes my desire scares me.
Sometimes I watch football
and think: four chances
is enough to get there. But
we don't have helmets.
I want to say harder,
I can take it, but
there's no proof I can.

Trying

ADA LIMÓN

I'd forgotten how much
I like to grow things, I shout
to him as he passes me to paint
the basement. I'm trellising
the tomatoes in what's called
a Florida weave. Later, we try
to knock me up again. We do it
in the guest room because that's
the extent of our adventurism
in a week of violence in Florida
and France. Afterwards,
the sun still strong though lowering
inevitably on the horizon, I check
on the plants in the back, my
fingers smelling of sex and tomato
vines. Even now, I don't know much
about happiness. I still worry
and want an endless stream of more,
but some days I can see the point
in growing something, even if
it's just to say I cared enough.

Christ You Delight Me

SANDRA CISNEROS

Christ you delight me,
Woolen scent of your sex,
Fury of your memory,
My hands still on the hilt
Of that excalibur of hip,
Blessed resurrection of thigh,
All these miles, *ay!*

Even now, as far away from you
As desert and mesa will allow,
Even now, under this welcome
Rain, yellow roses and honey-

Suckle vines, I have to hunker
My cunt close to the earth,
This little pendulum of mine
Ringing, ringing, ringing.

The Hummingbird: A Seduction

PATTIANN ROGERS

If I were a female hummingbird perched still
And quiet on an upper myrtle branch
In the spring afternoon and if you were a male
Alone in the whole heavens before me, having parted
Yourself, for me, from cedar top and honeysuckle stem
And earth down, your body hovering in midair
Far away from jewelweed, thistle, and bee balm;

And if I watched how you fell, plummeting before me,
And how you rose again and fell, with such mastery
That I believed for a moment *you* were the sky
And the red-marked bird diving inside your circumference
Was just the physical revelation of the light's
Most perfect desire;

And if I saw your sweeping and sucking
Performance of swirling egg and semen in the air,
The weaving, twisting vision of red petal
And nectar and soaring rump, the rush of your wing
In its grand confusion of arcing and splitting
Created completely out of nothing just for me,

Then when you came down to me, I would call you
My own spinning bloom of ruby sage, my funneling
Storm of sunlit sperm and pollen, my only breathless
Piece of scarlet sky, and I would bless the base
Of each of your feathers and touch the tine
Of string muscles binding your wings and taste

The odor of your glistening oils and hunt
The honey in your crimson flare
And I would take you and take you and take you
Deep into any kind of nest you ever wanted.

Seamless Beauty

WENDY LEE

The flower, the sky, your beloved, can only be
found in the present moment.
— Thich Nhat Hanh

Bittersweet, this lying under you,
your nose buried in my neck.
Can't get enough of your scent, you mumble,
and fall asleep.

I kiss the sweat-licked shiny top of your head
and twirl my finger slowly round and round
a lock of hair at the base of your neck.
Round and round, echoing the tug,
pull and swirling of our energies
which only moments ago, spun us out,
off this soft bed, careening to a place
where our joining felt infinite.

Someday I'd like to die this way
with you still inside me,
fall into a deep sleep and never wake up,
never have to know the parting,
the spent wave leaving the shore.

Your hair hugs my finger, and falls away.
Each twirl brings you closer yet farther from me.
The holding on becomes the letting go.

Downward

ERICA JONG

Because your eyes are the color of shadows on Chartres Cathedral
 because your sunglasses are smoke
  because smoke curls out of your ears to music
   because your mustache shades the letters of your words
    because your neck is planted in your shoulders
     because your tiny nipples rise to meet my tongue
      because the navel of your earth has never been discovered by Columbus
       because we are going downward

       Because the black hair whorls on your belly
        because your knees are mountain ranges
         because my mouth is a valley of melting snow
          because your penis is no metaphor
           because your thighs are horses galloping
            because your feet are the beginning & the beginning again
             because their soles tattoo the air
              because we are going we are going downward

Everything Depends Upon

JANE ANN DEVOL FULLER

Sex and how well we position ourselves,
the elbow developing a wing,
the reciprocating knee,
the bird at the window proving
all ledges are not for jumping—
sometimes perching, watching with great admiration
how a foot can be a part when it is nothing more than bone
and sometimes broken, what
I love about you is your body, how it moves
around your soul, a hand inside a glove, and when I see it
    bare
like this and wanting, I think how honey wants the bee
to come.

Eros at Temple Stream

DENISE LEVERTOV

The river in its abundance
many-voiced
all about us as we stood
on a warm rock to wash

slowly
smoothing in long
                    sliding strokes
our soapy hands along each other's
slippery cool bodies

quiet and slow in the midst of
the quick of the
sounding river

our hands were
flames
stealing upon quickened flesh until

no part of us but was
sleek and
on fire

The Best Seven Minutes of My Life

LORNA DEE CERVANTES

were spent with you. How many poems
open like that? How many yous open like that
to a touch? Your delicate face in my palms,
the blush of our truth on your cheeks. What sudden
love, yes, struck silly talking, a new you pressed
to my hips. We were a way out of that cul-de-sac
of our fin de siècle. We were a single wave
pushing into a shore—our lives, unfolding
before us: all the chip-lipped cups and the books,
the rats stacked up in cages, your instruments
and their cases completing the high-rise cityscape
in the kitchen. How I cooked for you, love
in the making, our love-making made permanent
in the stamping. Yes, I loved you. Yes, you were
the love of my life—that time. Yes, we were.
Though we never made that summit and made love
in a tent above treeline. I never stopped wanting
you. You, in all your delicate shards and ways,
curling to me, covering me with your boney
wires, all the you coming out of you,
all the ways to live and love in seven
minutes of wonder, and wounding, or less.

Afternoon

NINA RUBINSTEIN ALONSO

1.

One hot summer at midday
I lay down on the bed to rest,
One curtain in the bedroom shut,
But others partly open
To let in a soft broken light
Something like the light in woods,
Not twilight, really,
Not quite like the light before dawn,
But inbetween and shadowy,
Perfect for making love half-shy
When you want to see and be seen
Yet also half wish to be veiled, unknown.

2.

My love came in wearing loose clothes,
Looking in the light almost mythical,
A goddess coming to her lover's bed.
I began at the clothes
But she held them shut,
Scared for the moment, shivering,
A fright as if we had never made love,
As if she still were saying 'no'
The way she used to when she meant
'Yes' so terribly. Suddenly she let
The clothing go, her eyes changed
And she stopped trembling.

3.

Her body is so perfectly made
To discover the strength of love
Again and again, those strong thighs,
The tenderness of the shoulders,
The breasts and smooth belly!
The hunger hit us,
A heavy sweetness so intense
It is something like fainting
While leaping up in the air;
We touched and fell over
Moaning on the bed, praying
To each other for endless afternoons.

> *(after Christopher Marlowe's*
> *translation of the* Amore 1, 5
> *of Ovid)*

Curtains of Goldenrod

DIANE ACKERMAN

Where curtains of goldenrod, dry
after their season's stiff yellow plume,
made hilltop a chamber, and a dozen blues
like confluent rivers of sky, met,
there, beneath the wild hay, you took me,
on a horseblanket, in a polar month,
sun hot on our heels, as well as our brains,
turning me nimbly on forehand and haunch,
while jets passed over like breaking waves.
I have scratches where the straw weeds chafed;
you made me willow like the bending grain.
Above, your eyes looked bluer than two ermine
in winter, bluer than the day's high nape.
Even the sky seemed to begin with your face.

Capitulation

BARBARA GOLDBERG

And wouldn't we always slip
into the hot slick coat of it,
spurning food to feel our mouths
go dry with it, stretch out
our arms for this one's lust,
that one's need? We tremble
into being, take in the morning's
striking palette, our lips dusted

with the taste of it. Those sounds
we make, wouldn't they be torn out
by the root, and the wounds
suffered gladly? Anima, animus, we
descend into our evolutionary niche,
wild, demonic, from the bliss of it.

Buttons

CHERYL CLARKE

I wanted to unbutton every piece of your clothing
which was all buttons
from that silk shirt
down to the crotch of that gaberdine skirt.
My buttons too:
my jeans brass-button up,
my shirt has six shell buttons,
my camisole has three tiny ones.
This restaurant is in my way
when I want to be unbuttoned
and unbuttoning.
Can't you tell?
To do it now.
To reach across the bread.
To start unbuttoning.
My arms so long.
My fingers faster than the eye and omnidextrous.
Now, ain't that loving you?

green boy

KAI CHENG THOM

you spill
pollen and hayseed
all over me.
naked, i wear only
the grass stains
your fingers leave behind.
i want to go hunting for spring
in your body.
you open windows in mine.
my name in your mouth
is a pigeon, is a dove, is a canary
it circles the room—once, twice, three times
singing
then darts out the window
to light up the december night.

Housebound

AMY GERSTLER

When we fuck, stars don't peer down: they can't.
We fornicate indoors, under roofs, under wraps;
far from nature's prying eyes—from the trees'
slight green choreography, wrung from rigid trunks,
that leaves us unmoved. In full view of the shower
head and bookcases, we lick and tickle each other.
Every stick of furniture's a witness. We'd like
to believe our love's a private sentiment, yet
how many couches, cots, and benches have soaked up
some? Lust adheres to objects, becomes a prejudice
instilled in utensils by human use. How can I blind
these Peeping Toms—silence the libidinous whining
of these sipped-from paper cups and used toothbrushes?
I can't. I wait for the outspoken adolescent spoons
to rust and hold their tongues so we can be alone.

More or Less Love Poems #7

DIANE DI PRIMA

No aperture of your body I do not know
no way into your gut I have not studied

so now
we pause for this finesse
silk at your temples
and
in the hollow of your neck
a tongue
goes gently

I Love It When

SHARON OLDS

I love it when you roll over
and lie on me in the night, your weight
steady on me as tons of water, my
lungs like a little, shut box,
the firm, haired surface of your legs
opening my legs, my heart swells
to a taut purple boxing glove and then
sometimes I love to lie there doing
nothing, my powerful arms thrown down,
bolts of muslin rippling from the selvage,
your pubic bone a pyramid set
point down on the point of another
—glistening fulcrum. Then, in the stillness,
I love to feel you grow and grow be-
tween my legs like a plant in fast motion
the way, in the auditorium, in the
dark, near the beginning of our lives,
above us, the enormous stems and flowers
unfolded in silence.

Floating Islands

ENID SHOMER

The afternoon we swam nude
in the Gulf, the sun struck against the sky
like a brand slowly cooling,
the waves twinging apart as if they'd
learned modesty, I wanted to touch
his hips tapering in the murky
depth, and pick up the white shells
of his feet. I wanted my breasts
to bob free of the sea's plunging
neckline and taste his salty hair
and push it back and kiss his forehead and kiss
underwater on the lips, our breath
rising like columns of mercury,
his arms drifting around me
like strands of kelp. I wanted the water
to slow down his desire, I'd said,
so he'd know how a woman feels it,
more like a feather drawn
across the flesh than a flame. For an hour
we floated, two shy camellias
in a shallow blue bowl. We talked
and treaded and kept our distance.
But that night in the shower he pressed
one of his legs between mine and asked
could I pee right then so he'd know the slow
warm sensation down a woman's thighs.

Hold Back

ROBIN BECKER

Like afternoon shadows on October adobes, she will fall
    and fall on me, wind fluttering white at the window,
        smell of piñon fires and first snow

on the mountain. Cool blue altitudes we drive,
    down here we burn, let silence rain its quiet
        weather, let her suntanned arm graze mine

with its peachbloom glaze; I know how to walk away
    and come back shining. In time she will open her shirt,
        she will show me her neck, she will close her eyes.

But we're not yet lovers, we're seekers from the valleys,
    laden with turquoise and silver, interested
        in each other the way traders fall in love

with a beautiful bracelet, the one they haven't had
    and still think will make a difference. But we're not
        thinking of the future—that's one of the conditions—

I'm tracing her palm with my finger and feeling
    the Rio Grande rush over the autumn stones. I'm kissing
        the inside of her elbow, the moccasin-soft skin

is a song I heard at the pueblo when the women
    danced together the small, mysterious movements.
        Soon she'll lie on her stomach with her chest pressed

into the thin sheet and I'll climb
    to her back, freckled with summer
        light. Impatient, she throws her head left and right,

she wants me to begin, she's been waiting
        all afternoon for my hand
                at the base of her spine,

so I hold back. All we know of pleasure
        is pleasure delayed, the fine
                restraint which once given over is gone.

I Live My Life by Three Minute Phone Calls

LAURA BOSS

I live my life by three minute phone calls
strange booths—smelling of stale urine
dirty gum on the floor
dropped often quarters stay on the ground
I'm showered and ready to go
but still I close the doors
though most glass booths
are now open phone booths
only down to the waist
I'm searching for an old wooden one
privacy
can you touch yourself? you ask
I look around the open shopping center
and wish for the dusky dark phone booths
in the back of a nowhere
in the warmth
out of the outdoors
once I cut holes in my coat pockets
found a deserted booth at night
glass that lit up when the door closed
left the door open
but I couldn't seem to focus between my legs
standing up
I wanted to go home—cars going by
call me at home, I plead
too dangerous, you say
I want to forget the phone booths
at 7-11, at the Acme, at the shopping malls
I want to phone you and hear you tell me

to hang up
and drive through the darkness
through the tunnel
to your place.

In Celebration

Last night I licked
your love, you love,
like a cat. And
I watched you rise like
bread baking, like
a helium balloon, rise
with the skill of a soufflé,
your love, waving like
passengers on a boat coming in.
My cheek resting on your belly,
moist like a bathroom mirror, resting
in your hair like
dew grass, I drew
your love out like
the head of a turtle, like
an accordion, like
an expandable drinking glass.
I licked,
you love, your love,
hard as a lollipop, plump
and tender as a plum.
I held you
like a mitten, like a cup,
and, like the crowds in the spray of a Yellowstone geyser,
like kids splashing in a July fire hydrant,
like a dinner guest biting in a whole tomato,
I gasped,
I laughed,
I feasted on your vintage.

Something Like Rivers Ran

SANDRA CISNEROS

undid the knot the ribbons
    the silk flags of motion
unraveled from under

the flesh of the wrists
    the stone of the lungs
something like water

broke free the prayer
    of the heart
the grief of the hands

crooned sweet when
    you held me
dissolved knee into knee

belly into belly
    an alphabet of limbs
ran urgently

nudged loose a pebble
    a pearl
a noose undoing its greed

and we were Buddha
    and we were Jesus
and we were Allah

at once
    a Ganges absolving
language woman man

On a night of the full moon

AUDRE LORDE

I

Out of my flesh that hungers
and my mouth that knows
comes the shape I am seeking
for reason.
The curve of your waiting body
fits my waiting hand
your breasts warm as sunlight
your lips quick as young birds
between your thighs the sweet
sharp taste of limes.

Thus I hold you
frank in my heart's eye
in my skin's knowing
as my fingers conceive your flesh
I feel your stomach
curving against me.

Before the moon wanes again
we shall come together.

II

And I would be the moon
spoken over your beckoning flesh
breaking against reservations
beaching thought
my hands at your high tide

over and under inside you
and the passing of hungers
attended, forgotten.

Darkly risen
the moon speaks
my eyes
judging your roundness
delightful.

This Corner of the Western World

JENNIFER CHANG

Dark thing,
make a myth of yourself:

all women turn into lilacs,

all men grow sick of their errant scent.
You could learn

to build a window, to change flesh
into isinglass, nothing

but a brittle river, a love of bone.

You could snap like a branch—*No,*

this way, he says, and the fence
releases the forest,

and every blue insect finds an inch of skin.
He loves low voices, diffidence

on the invented trail,

the stones you fuck him on. Yes
to sweat's souvenir, yes to his fist

in your hair, you bite

because you can. Silence
rides the back of your throat,

his tongue, your name.

Amazon Twins

OLGA BROUMAS

I.

You wanted to compare, and there
we were, eyes on each eye, the lower
lids
squinting
suddenly awake

though the light was dim.   Looking away
some time ago, you'd said
   the eyes are live
   animals, domiciled in our head
but more than the head

is crustacean-like.   Marine
eyes, marine
odors.   Everything live
(tongue, clitoris, lip and lip)
swells in its moist shell.   I remember the light

warped round our bodies finally
crustal, striated with sweat.

II.

In the gazebo-like café, you gave
me food from your plate, alert
to my blood-sweet hungers
double edged
in the glare of the sun's

and our own
twin heat.   Yes, there

we were, breasts on each side, Amazons
adolescent at twentynine
privileged
to keep the bulbs and to feel the blade
swell, breath-sharp
on either side.   In that public place

in that public place.

The Sad Truth

ELLEN BASS

My lover is a woman. I cherish
her sex—the puffy lips of the vulva
like ripe apricot halves, the thin inner lips
that lie closed, gently as eyelids.
I love the slippery slide up her
vagina and the whole thing thrown open
like a Casa Blanca lily. I savor her
taste and smell and how easily she can
pop out one lovely orgasm after another
like a baker turning out loaves of fragrant bread.
Sixteen years and I haven't grown tired
of that oasis, that mouth watering hole.
Yet sometimes, I do miss a penis,
that nice thick flesh that hardens
to just the right consistency. I miss
feeling it nudge me from behind in the night,
poking in between my legs. And the way it goes
out ahead, an envoy, blatant and exposed
on the open plain. It's so easy
to get its attention.
It jumps up in greeting like a setter.
And I'd enjoy it stuffed inside me
like a big wad of money in a purse.
I don't want another lover, but
sometimes I recall it. That longing
grabs me by the waist, dips me back,
sweeps my hair across the polished floor.

2 AM

DORIANNE LAUX

When I came with you that first time
on the floor of your office, the dirty carpet
under my back, the heel of one foot
propped on your shoulder, I went ahead
and screamed, full-throated, as loud
and as long as my body demanded,
because somewhere, in the back of my mind,
packed in the smallest neurons still capable
of thought, I remembered
we were in a warehouse district
and that no sentient being resided for miles.
Afterwards, when I could unclench
my hands and open my eyes, I looked up.
You were on your knees, your arms
stranded at your sides, so still—
the light from the crooknecked lamp
sculpting each lift and delicate twist,
the lax muscles, the smallest veins
on the backs of your hands. I saw
the ridge of each rib, the blue hollow
pulsing at your throat, all the colors
in your long blunt cut hair which hung
over your face like a raffia curtain
in some south sea island hut.
And as each bright synapse unfurled
and followed its path, I recalled
a story I'd read that explained why women
cry out when they come—that it's
the call of the conqueror, a siren howl

of possession. So I looked again
and it felt true, your whole body
seemed defeated, owned, having taken on
the aspect of a slave in shackles, the wrists
loosely bound with invisible rope.
And when you finally spoke you didn't
lift your head but simply moaned the word *god*
on an exhalation of breath—I knew then
I must be merciful, benevolent,
impossibly kind.

(The Floating Poem, Unnumbered)*

ADRIENNE RICH

Whatever happens with us, your body
will haunt mine—tender, delicate
your lovemaking, like the half-curled frond
of the fiddlehead fern in forests
just washed by sun. Your traveled, generous thighs
between which my whole face has come and come—
the innocence and wisdom of the place my tongue has found
    there—
the live, insatiate dance of your nipples in my mouth—
your touch on me, firm, protective, searching
me out, your strong tongue and slender fingers
reaching where I had been waiting years for you
in my rose-wet cave—whatever happens, this is.

*From "Twenty-One Love Poems"

Blindfolds, Ropes

SHERYL ST. GERMAIN

In this place of utter light and vastness
I have lit my soul with searchlights,
and cannot tell the limits of my fear or joy.

The truth is I miss your blindfolds and ropes,
those gifts I left with you.

In light you are gangly and red-nosed,
in dark you become the Beloved—
all breath, skin and tongue—
a truth no light would reveal.

Tonight when I close my eyes
the sky will fill with lovers
binding the wrists of lovers,
the night will tie its blindfold
over the earth's eyes, and I will
dream of how to speak—oh

kiss me with lips I have to imagine;
hold me in a room I can't escape.

I Have No Use for Virgins

JANE HIRSHFIELD

I have no use for virgins—
give me the cup
with a chipped lip,
whose handle is glued back on
and whose glaze is dark from use.
Let many men and women
drink from us before
we drink—
I taste their breasts on your breast,
you cover their blaze between my legs.

PART III

When

This Old Body

Gate C22

ELLEN BASS

At gate C22 in the Portland airport
a man in a broad-band leather hat kissed
a woman arriving from Orange County.
They kissed and kissed and kissed. Long after
the other passengers clicked the handles of their carry-ons
and wheeled briskly toward short-term parking,
the couple stood there, arms wrapped around each other
like he'd just staggered off the boat at Ellis Island,
like she'd been released at last from ICU, snapped
out of a coma, survived bone cancer, made it down
from Annapurna in only the clothes she was wearing.

Neither of them was young. His beard was gray.
She carried a few extra pounds you could imagine
her saying she had to lose. But they kissed lavish
kisses like the ocean in the early morning,
the way it gathers and swells, sucking
each rock under, swallowing it
again and again. We were all watching—
passengers waiting for the delayed flight
to San Jose, the stewardesses, the pilots,
the aproned woman icing Cinnabons, the man selling
sunglasses. We couldn't look away. We could
taste the kisses crushed in our mouths.

But the best part was his face. When he drew back
and looked at her, his smile soft with wonder, almost
as though he were a mother still open from giving birth,
as your mother must have looked at you, no matter

what happened after—if she beat you or left you or
you're lonely now—you once lay there, the vernix
not yet wiped off, and someone gazed at you
as if you were the first sunrise seen from the Earth.
The whole wing of the airport hushed,
all of us trying to slip into that woman's middle-aged body,
her plaid Bermuda shorts, sleeveless blouse, glasses,
little gold hoop earrings, tilting our heads up.

What Humans Do

WENDY VIDELOCK

The candlelit
after-dinner
careful screw,

the under-the-moon
shooby doo
be doo groove,

the from behind,
the sixty-nine,
the *is there time*,

the *I need wine*,
the twisted talking
dirty grind,

the Erica Jong
zipless screw,
the I-got-somethin'-

to-prove ruse,
the primal bang,
the power game,

the long play,
the itchy-ish, sudden-ish
roll in the hay,

the *take me away*,
the once a month
married way,

the hail mary,
the holy-joe-
I-can't-believe-

my-luck hump,
the side to side
slow pump,

the grudge fuck,
the quick poke,
the hard core,

the tenderest lap
of waves on the shore,
and the gushing rushing

endless coming
of *I've never felt
this way before.*

Kisses

KIM ADDONIZIO

All the kisses I've ever been given, today I feel them on my
    mouth.
And my knees feel them, the reckless ones placed there
through the holes in my jeans while I sat on a car hood
or a broken sofa in somebody's basement, stoned, the way I
    was
in those days, still amazed that boys and even men would
    want to
lower their beautiful heads like horses drinking from a river
    and taste me.
The back of my neck feels them, my hair swept aside to
    expose the nape,
and my breasts tingle the way they did when my milk came in
    after the birth,
when I was swollen, and sleepless, and my daughter fed and
    fed until I pried
her from me and laid her in her crib. Even the chaste kisses
    that brushed
my cheeks, the fatherly ones on my forehead, I feel them
    rising up from underneath
the skin of the past, a delicate, roseate rash; and the ravishing
    ones, God,
I think of them and the filaments in my brain start buzzing
    crazily and flare out.
Every kiss is here somewhere, all over me like a fine, shiny
    grit, like I'm a pale
fish that's been dipped in a thick swirl of raw egg and
    dragged through flour,

slid down into a deep skillet, into burning. Today I know I've
  lost no one.
My loves are here: wrists, eyelids, damp toes, all scars, and
  my mouth
pouring praises, still asking, saying *kiss me*; when I'm dead
  kiss this poem,
it needs you to know it goes on, give it your lovely mouth,
  your living tongue.

Your Fingers Are Still

CHRYSTOS

inside me pulsing
as I vacuum   look at books   wash dishes   cook
ride down the road   open my mail   burn the trash
Your fingers buckle
my knees   Stomach turns over   small moans
escape my lips at the laundromat   grocery store
Your tongue shivering me while I call a new job
pull the covers up on my bed   go to the bank
Smack of your comforting belly as you come on me
as I catch a ferry   iron a shirt   pull weeds
Your fingers don't stop
moving me

Wet

CAROLYN CREEDON

I want to leak all over the world,
the wet and tilted wheel, to squat in its axis
and spit my slippery fish, red and gasping
on the asphalt, under the streetlight. I want my life
streaked down my leg, to rain my seed on the ground
like a wine's sooty dregs. I want you to see that I am who
I say I am, an unsavory woman with her seasons undone. I
    want to lay
you, on a bed without a towel, without a curtain, without a
    good enough
reason. I want to wear a white dress stained with certain
    possibility, like an autograph,
like a river ripe with spawn, like a signpost, like a season,
like a dam come all undone.

Love Poem

AUDRE LORDE

Speak earth and bless me with what is richest
make sky flow honey out of my hips
rigid as mountains
spread over a valley
carved out by the mouth of rain.

And I knew when I entered her I was
high wind in her forests hollow
fingers whispering sound
honey flowed
from the split cup
impaled on a lance of tongues
on the tips of her breasts on her navel
and my breath
howling into her entrances
through lungs of pain.

Greedy as herring-gulls
or a child
I swing out over the earth
over and over
again.

Phenomenal Woman

MAYA ANGELOU

Pretty women wonder where my secret lies.
I'm not cute or built to suit a fashion model's size
But when I start to tell them,
They think I'm telling lies.
I say,
It's in the reach of my arms,
The span of my hips,
The stride of my step,
The curl of my lips.
I'm a woman
Phenomenally.
Phenomenal woman,
That's me.

I walk into a room
Just as cool as you please,
And to a man,
The fellows stand or
Fall down on their knees.
Then they swarm around me,
A hive of honey bees.
I say,
It's the fire in my eyes,
And the flash of my teeth,
The swing in my waist,
And the joy in my feet.
I'm a woman
Phenomenally.
Phenomenal woman,
That's me.

Men themselves have wondered
What they see in me.
They try so much
But they can't touch
My inner mystery.
When I try to show them,
They say they still can't see.
I say,
It's in the arch of my back,
The sun of my smile,
The ride of my breasts,
The grace of my style.
I'm a woman
Phenomenally.
Phenomenal woman,
That's me.

Now you understand
Just why my head's not bowed.
I don't shout or jump about
Or have to talk real loud.
When you see me passing,
It ought to make you proud.
I say,
It's in the click of my heels,
The bend of my hair,
the palm of my hand,
The need for my care.
'Cause I'm a woman
Phenomenally.
Phenomenal woman,
That's me.

homage to my hips

LUCILLE CLIFTON

these hips are big hips
they need space to
move around in.
they don't fit into little
petty places. these hips
are free hips.
they don't like to be held back.
these hips have never been enslaved,
they go where they want to go
they do what they want to do.
these hips are mighty hips.
these hips are magic hips.
i have known them
to put a spell on a man and
spin him like a top!

Freed Up

WENDY BARKER

He said I had nice ones, even though I'd always thought they were so little, but why did I bind them up? One day I left my bra in the drawer. All day could feel the feel of them. Couldn't forget they were there. Felt good just leaning down to throw a wad of paper in the trash. And standing up, nipples like third and fourth eyes, looking straight out at whoever was coming toward me in the long hall. Looking clear inside. Into secrets, hiding places. Until they were out for good, out of the muffled fiber-filled shells, elastic tightenings, hard-wire frames. Like bare green leaves unfolding in April, swelling as they opened. Leisurely, soft, brushing into a hand.

To Endings

KATHERINE RIEGEL

I believe Icarus was not failing as he fell,
but just coming to the end of his triumph.
—*Jack Gilbert*

There's a guy ordering hot chocolate at the counter
and when the barista asks him
if he wants whipped cream he says
yeah in this low, breathy voice that tells everyone
he *always* wants whipped cream and don't all of us,
really? If I notice things like that too often or
too keenly now, is that a bad thing, or just slightly
less appealing, like hot chocolate *without* whipped
cream—still good, rich and mouthy, but not quite
everything you wanted? Anyway I care less
and less about appropriate and more and more
about wanting, about moans and sighs and how the sound
of a zipper can make you want to lie down
right where you are—on the sidewalk even, with
the cigarette butts and the cold seeping into your back,
if only someone would just kiss you
like they do in the movies. And I care
about beginnings, the lips finding that spot
on the neck, the too-much-clothing between skin
and skin; even more, perhaps, about middles'
secret stories, the slow but firm
touch, the nightingale vines curling from open mouths
into the dark. And when the ending finally
comes, the song trilled out to its last fluid note,
do we call that failure?

Marriage Without Sex

ELLEN BASS

I don't know how people stay married
without sex. How they can stand their mates
day in, day out, the irritations grating
like sand under the band of your bathing suit
when you're sunburned and greasy and one kid
doesn't want to leave and the other one's crabbing,
there's no more juice and too much to carry to the car.
How could they tolerate it
week after week—the way he does the laundry,
mixing darks and lights, how he dangles
spaghetti from his mouth and chomps
along the strands like a cow, or when she
repeats what she read in the paper, as though
she thought of it herself, doesn't answer
when he speaks, or gets lost
going someplace she's been twenty times before.
How can couples bear
each other without the glory
of their bodies rising up like whales, breaking
the surface in a glossy arc,
finding each other in the long smooth flanks,
hidden coves, the gift of sound rushing
from their throats like spray.
What could make them appreciate
each other enough to stay without
this ocean that smooths the crumpled beach,
leveling the ground again.

Four Beginnings / for Kyra

OLGA BROUMAS

1. You raise
   your face from mine, parting
   my breath like water, hair falling
   away in its own wind, and your eyes—
   green in the light like honey—surfacing
   on my body, awed
   with desire, speechless, this common dream.

2. You bore your marriage like a misconceived
   animal, and have the scars, the pale
   ridged tissue round front and back
   for proof.   For proof.   Tonight

   we cross into each other's language.   I take your hand
   hesitant still with regret
   into that milky landscape, where braille
   is a tongue for lovers, where tongue,
   fingers, lips
   share a lidless eye.

3. I was surprised myself—the image of the lithe
   hermaphroditic lover a staple of
   every fantasy, bought, borrowed, or mine.   We never did
   mention the word, unqualified: I love:
   your hair, I love: your feet, toes, tender nibbles, I love:
   I love.   You are the memory
   of each desire that ran, dead-end, into a mind
   programmed to misconstrue it.   A mind inventing
   neurosis, anxiety, phobia, a mind expertly camouflaged

from the thought of love
for a woman, its native
love.

4. I in my narrow body, spellbound
against your flesh.

the wounded for healing

KAI CHENG THOM

you push your mouth against mine
i want to tell you
you have come to the wounded for healing.
like you, i am
imperfect flesh, and my
experience of violence has made me
no less likely to harm you.
history is doomed
to repeat itself
colonization and rape
are written on my bones.
i want to tell you
i am trying. like you, i
have come to the wounded for healing. we
are two scars pressed together, trying
to give birth to new skins.

The animal kingdom

MARGE PIERCY

In bed our bodies mutate.
We have many small supple bones
so we can coil round each other
warm blooded serpents slithering
twisting, skin dancing on skin.

In bed our bodies change.
Wings poke through our shoulder
blades and open umbrellalike
and then we beat up to the ceiling,
we rise through the roof,

we soar into obsidian night
then dive clutched like falcons,
talons interlocked, the wind
beating in our hot blood
as we shriek our razor sharp joy.

In bed we are small and cosy,
mice in a nest of feathers.
We purr like kittens tumbling
over each other's furry flanks
and nipping with sharp teeth.

In bed we act the grace
of dolphins arcing like a wheel,
the grace of water falling
from a cliff white and sparkling
in a roar of spume.

In a moment we will be our
mundane selves flopping in a net
of unpaid bills and Things that Must
be Done, and aren't, email,
grocery lists and fungoid nails.

But now we are stately giraffes
nibbling the high browse of fore
heads; tigers stalking our sweet
prey through pubic jungles; lords
of the animal kingdom of sex.

Drowning in Paradise

ADA LIMÓN

The low hanging hibiscus coos out
its swollen-mouth flower song
to the rare bee holding its tongue
and I'm drunk on the bully world again—
a filed up fluster coming on.
Look, even two oceans can collide
here in the belly of white islands.
Splurge and risk in the conch-dark
night—I'm going to walk into the water's
frothy rim. Come here shark. Come
here barracuda. Love the sweet artifacts
of this body. Carry me in the world-class
rattle of a wave. I want the big bite, one
restless, tooth-filled mouth to take me down.

Dulzura

SANDRA CISNEROS

Make love to me in Spanish.
Not with that other tongue.
I want you *juntito a mí*,
tender like the language
crooned to babies.
I want to be that
lullabied, *mi bien*
querido, that loved.

I want you inside
the mouth of my heart,
inside the harp of my wrists,
the sweet meat of the mango,
in the gold that dangles
from my ears and neck.

Say my name. Say it.
The way it's supposed to be said.
I want to know that I knew you
even before I knew you.

Ecstasy

SHARON OLDS

As we made love for the third day,
cloudy and dark, as we did not stop
but went into it and into it and
did not hesitate and did not hold back we
rose through the air, until we were up above
timber line. The lake lay
icy and silver, the surface shirred,
reflecting nothing. The black rocks
lifted around it into the grainy
sepia air, the patches of snow
brilliant white, and even though we
did not know where we were, we could not
speak the language, we could hardly see, we
did not stop, rising with the black
rocks to the black hills, the black
mountains rising from the hills. Resting
on the crest of the mountains, one huge
cloud with scalloped edges of blazing
evening light, we did not turn back,
we stayed with it, even though we were
far beyond what we knew, we rose
into the grain of the cloud, even though we were
frightened, the air hollow, even though
nothing grew there, even though it is a
place from which no one has ever come back.

After Love

MAXINE KUMIN

Afterwards, the compromise.
Bodies resume their boundaries.

These legs, for instance, mine.
Your arms take you back in.

Spoons of our fingers, lips
admit their ownership.

The bedding yawns, a door
blows aimlessly ajar

and overhead, a plane
singsongs coming down.

Nothing is changed, except
there was a moment when

the wolf, the mongering wolf
who stands outside the self

lay lightly down, and slept.

Afterwards

DORIANNE LAUX

when we sat side by side
on the edge of the unmade bed,
staring blindly at our knees, our feet,
our clothes stranded in the middle of the floor
like small, crumpled islands,
you put your arm around my shoulder
in that gesture usually reserved
for those of the same sex—equals,
friends, as if we'd
accomplished something together,
like climbing a hill or painting a house,
your hand at rest over the curved bone
of my shoulder, my loud nipples
softening into sleep.
Stripped of our want, our wildness, we sat
naked and tired and companionable
in the sleek silence, innocent
of what we'd said, what we'd done,
our breath slowing, our heads tipped
and touching at the crown,
like a couple of kids
slumped on a dock in the sun, our legs
dangling above the bright water,
admiring each other's reflections.

Watching You in the Mirror

ALICE FRIMAN

Suppose I stood behind you,
slipped my bare arms under yours
and arced them about, making you
into a four-armed god, all ministering
to your fresh-from-the-shower nakedness—
combing, deodorizing, touching
toothpaste to your brush—while you
concentrated on shaving, twisting
your mouth in that funny way you do.

Would you, compelled
by the light streaming in the window,
lift up one foot as if to dance—toes flexed,
heel down—and balancing on one leg,
glow as Shiva did in that ring of fire?

And if I suddenly bit you
the way I do sometimes, and you
unable to turn, caught in the bas-
relief of the game, how would you
read me? I have played wife
so well for fifteen years. Turban-
wrapped behind you, my name, Surya,
copper-headed daughter of the sun
who, like my father roaring in the ether,
loves to linger over skin, using her teeth
to know you. The gods say death comes only
to those who blink. Gods never blink

or shut their eyes, but shuffle the world,
growing tusks long with knowledge.

Husband, I tell you, there will be no end
to my knowing. In the reflection of my eyes,
you shall never sleep. If necessary, I will
gnaw each mirror you're in, swallowing
it down to keep you awake and inside me.

Of Gravity & Angels

JANE HIRSHFIELD

And suddenly, again,
I want the long road of your thigh
under my hand, your well-traveled thigh,
your salt-slicked & come-slicked thigh,
and I want the taste of you, slaking,
under my tongue (that place of riding desire,
my tongue) and I want
all the unnameable, soft, and yielding places,
belly & neck & the place wings would rise from
if we were angels,
and we are, and I want the rising regions of you
shoulder & cock & tongue & breathing &
suddenness of you
opening
all fontanel, all desire, the whole thing beginning
for the first time again, the first,
until I wonder then how is it
we even know which part we are,
even know the ground that lifts us, raucous,
out of ourselves,
as the rising sound of a summer dawn
when all of it joins in.

Integrity

LORNA DEE CERVANTES

Yours is the integrity of flint,
of steel, of iron. Yours
is the integrity of birds flocking,
whales in their loving pods. Yours
is the integrity of sand, what moves
with the will of you; all your sweet
sweat, your simple construction.
I love the sudden fill of you, your
swell and sway. I love how you do
what you say. You slay me
with your truth. I love the way
we fit together as if I were your
seed. I love the far away look
in your multicolored eyes, the land
and sea of you. I love
the way you look at me, that ancient
shore. I love how I am more
with you, your carbon, the filaments
of your fine hair. I love how you hold
me together, how fast and vast
the ocean of this love in its gentle
tide, the integrity of flesh, of salt,
of we.

Searching for the Comet

DIANE ACKERMAN

In the bright night of stars, they stood
on a wooden deck behind the bungalow,
searching for the comet that would appear
in tailless mastery through the open neck
of the Milky Way, blazing out
only to return to emptiness,
but in between riveting the sky with fire.
His arm arced around her waist,
they stood watching the crystal blackness
and the pinprick light of suns, thinking:
oh, the freedom of the day that yielded
to no rule or time, a day flung
from the orbit of their lives,
in which they drank from the well
of kisses for hours, set brush fires
in each other's limbs, and soared
above the flat world they mapped
with families a continent away,
oh, the cool compress of the evening,
the staggering fires of the day.

Us

ANNE SEXTON

I was wrapped in black
fur and white fur and
you undid me and then
you placed me in gold light
and then you crowned me,
while snow fell outside
the door in diagonal darts.
While a ten-inch snow
came down like stars
in small calcium fragments,
we were in our own bodies
(that room that will bury us)
and you were in my body
(that room that will outlive us)
and at first I rubbed your
feet dry with a towel
because I was your slave
and then you called me princess.
Princess!

Oh then
I stood up in my gold skin
and I beat down the psalms
and I beat down the clothes
and you undid the bridle
and you undid the reins
and I undid the buttons,
the bones, the confusions,

the New England postcards,
the January ten o'clock night,
and we rose up like wheat,
acre after acre of gold,
and we harvested,
we harvested.

Summer Solstice

STACIE CASSARINO

I wanted to see where beauty comes from
without you in the world, hauling my heart
across sixty acres of northeast meadow,
my pockets filling with flowers.
Then I remembered,
it's you I miss in the brightness
and body of every living name:
rattlebox, yarrow, wild vetch.
You are the green wonder of June,
root and quasar, the thirst for salt.
When I finally understand that people fail
at love, what is left but cinquefoil, thistle,
the paper wings of the dragonfly
aeroplaning the soul with a sudden blue hilarity?
If I get the story right, desire is continuous,
equatorial. There is still so much
I want to know: what you believe
can never be removed from us,
what you dreamed on Walnut Street
in the unanswerable dark of your childhood,
learning pleasure on your own.
Tell me our story: are we impetuous,
are we kind to each other, do we surrender
to what the mind cannot think past?
Where is the evidence I will learn
to be good at loving?
The black dog orbits the horseshoe pond
for treefrogs in their plangent emergencies.
There are violet hills,

there is the covenant of duskbirds.
The moon comes over the mountain
like a big peach, and I want to tell you
what I couldn't say the night we rushed
North, how I love the seriousness of your fingers
and the way you go into yourself,
calling my half-name like a secret.
I stand between taproot and treespire.
Here is the compass rose
to help me live through this.
Here are twelve ways of knowing
what blooms even in the blindness
of such longing. Yellow oxeye,
viper's bugloss with its set of pink arms
pleading do not forget me.
We hunger for eloquence.
We measure the isopleths.
I am visiting my life with reckless plenitude.
The air is fragrant with tiny strawberries.
Fireflies turn on their electric wills:
an effulgence. Let me come back
whole, let me remember how to touch you
before it is too late.

Song of the Current at Cape Horn

DIANE ACKERMAN

III

Come ride the fish-bright
  swells of my flesh
and lay-by in my limbs,
  greener than a glade.
Run aground, sailor,
  in my dark, tussocked eyes
swing round your mizzen,
  shipwreck in my thighs.

Only, come to my harbor.
  Sweet is the port air.
Time will drop its sail
  like a clipper in a lagoon.

There's a berth in my hips
  as wide as the moon,
a ribcage roomier than the sea,
  and here, awash
between outcry and the deep blue,
  my plunging heart
will fathom life from you.

We Thought of Each Other as Food

ROBIN BECKER

—*after David Shapiro*

We thought of each other as food, taut skin,
of the apple burnished with stars We thought of each other
as France, Brittany blue and Provençal roads, postcards
from the vast Midi of your mouth We thought of each other
as fact, a fanlight above the boathouse door
and then the door opened and we sailed
in the parallel hulls of feminine
endings, catamaran, raft of logs lashed together
We thought of each other as fish in fathoms of light
where we glistened and swam, in the dangerous rooms
and coral reefs where sea horses glittered
If I thought at all, my God, how could I
think when your hips churned, while the presses ran,
while someone on the night shift took a break
and stared at the summer constellations,
hovering like a map of the rest of her life?
We thought of each other as fiction
and wrote our story with kisses,
our characters spoke and revised their opinions,
each night they broke free from convention
We thought of each other as Ferris wheel and fairground
on the turning axes of our bodies

mary

LUCILLE CLIFTON

this kiss
as soft as cotton

over my breasts
all shiny bright

something is in this night
oh Lord have mercy on me

i feel a garden
in my mouth

between my legs
i see a tree

3. The Encounter*

LOUISE GLÜCK

You came to the side of the bed
and sat staring at me.
Then you kissed me—I felt
hot wax on my forehead.
I wanted it to leave a mark:
that's how I knew I loved you.
Because I wanted to be burned, stamped,
to have something in the end—
I drew the gown over my head;
a red flush covered my face and shoulders.
It will run its course, the course of fire,
setting a cold coin on the forehead, between the eyes.
You lay beside me; your hand moved over my face
as though you had felt it also—
you must have known, then, how I wanted you.
We will always know that, you and I.
The proof will be my body.

*From "Marathon"

Foreshadows

BARBARA GOLDBERG

Now that I've read
the first draft of your body
I can already tell
the rough places
where there is need
for further exploration.
In due time the clenched
jaws will release a flurry
of words, unearthing
the grave heart
from its vault of ribs.
And since there already is
perfection, the soft mounds
of your fingers, the exquisite
way they interpret my spine,
well then, I can wait
for the rest, the story
your tongue will tell
to the flesh and its slow unfolding.

The Return

MOLLY PEACOCK

When I open my legs to let you seek,
seek inside me, seeking more, I think
"What are you looking for?" and feel it will
be hid from me, whatever it is, still
or rapidly moving beyond my frequency.
Then I declare you a mystery
and stop myself from moving and hold still
until you can find your orgasm. Peak
is partly what you look for, and the brink
you love to come to and return to must
be part of it, too, thrust, build, the trust
that brings me, surprised, to a brink of my own . . .
I must be blind to something of my own
you recognize and look for. A diamond
speaks in a way through its beams, though it's dumb
to the brilliance it reflects. A gem at the back
of the cave must tell you, "Yes, you can go back."

The Long Tunnel of Wanting You

ERICA JONG

This is the long tunnel of wanting you.
Its walls are lined with remembered kisses
wet & red as the inside of your mouth,
full & juicy as your probing tongue,
warm as your belly against mine,
deep as your navel leading home,
soft as your sleeping cock beginning to stir,
tight as your legs wrapped around mine,
straight as your toes pointing toward the bed
as you roll over & thrust your hardness
into the long tunnel of my wanting,
seeding it with dreams & unbearable hope,
making memories of the future,
straightening out my crooked past,
teaching me to live in the present present tense
with the past perfect and the uncertain future
suddenly certain for certain
in the long tunnel of my old wanting
which before always had an ending
but now begins & begins again
with you, with you, with you.

Making Love to You When You're Far Away

ALISON HAWTHORNE DEMING

Sometimes it starts with words,
like when you're jammed
with work and have no time
and I say to myself, Baby,
there's always time for love,
and you take me then,
miles away and buzzed on
a thousand decisions about
windows or doors or cement,
and I do it myself with you
in mind and it's almost as
sweet as if you were there,
until it's over and you're not.

Sometimes it's a memory, say,
your graceful return that time
I threw something glib at you
and learned how substantial
you could be when I didn't
even know I needed that, but
I did, the way I need it now,
the thing you would give me
that I could not anticipate,
the lack I could not feel
until you replaced it with
something present. I want
to tell you the truth
without scaring you away.

Sometimes I think of love
as a dangerous storm
that makes me hunker down
in a powerless house
beside a flame too small
to keep me warm. I have been
reading the history of my problems
with men for as long as
I have been living it,
looking for the lessons
that would let me graduate
from the hard-knocks school of love—
no more painful requirements to fulfill
once I master the practice.

Today it started right here
on the page, hearing my voice
as if I were Penelope,
past anger, just waiting
and working in the dark, and
I had to leave my desk,
getting lost in you again,
both of us coming to a place
we had never been before,
a place we wanted to stay. What woman
can say she doesn't want
the moment in the myth when
Psyche lights the lamp,
unable to resist any longer
seeing what has been forbidden?

Feasting

ELIZABETH W. GARBER

I am so amazed to find myself kissing you
with such abandon,
filling myself with our kisses
astounding hunger for edges of lips and tongue.
Returning to feast again and again,
our bellies never overfilling from this banquet.
Returning in surprise,
in remembering,
in rediscovering,
such play of flavors of gliding lips
and forests of pressures and spaces.
The spaces between the branches
as delicious as finding the grove of lilies of the valley
blossoming just outside my door under the ancient oak.
"I've never held anyone this long," you said,
the second time you entered my kitchen.
I am the feast this kitchen was blessed to prepare
waiting for you to enter open mouthed in awe
in the mystery we've been given,
our holy feast.

God/Love Poem

LENORE KANDEL

there are no ways of love but/beautiful/
        I love you all of them

I love you / your cock in my hand
        stirs like a bird
in my fingers
as you swell and grow hard in my hand
forcing my fingers open
with your rigid strength
you are beautiful / you are beautiful
you are a hundred times beautiful
I stroke you with my loving hands
        pink-nailed long fingers
I caress you
I adore you
my finger-tips . . . my palms . . .
your cock rises and throbs in my hands
a revelation / as Aphrodite knew it

        there was a time when gods were purer
        /I can recall nights among the honeysuckle
        our juices sweeter than honey
        / we were the temple and the god entire/

I am naked against you
and I put my mouth on you   slowly
I have longing to kiss you
and my tongue makes worship on you
you are beautiful

your body moves to me
flesh to flesh
skin sliding over golden skin
as mine to yours
   my mouth   my tongue   my hands
my belly and my legs
against your mouth   your love
sliding . . . sliding . . .
our bodies move and join
unbearably

your face above me
   is the face of all the gods
     and beautiful demons
your eyes . . .

     love touches love
     the temple and the god
     are one

Doomsday

MAURYA SIMON

Slowly, like a hot tear tracing the skin's folds,
God drew His finger along my parted lips,

Then down, down along the round swelling of my chin,
Then slowly He skimmed my curved nape of neck—

Soft as a dove's throat and bare of any scent—
Turning delicately around my wingless collarbones,

His finger pulled its burning torch down to my breast
That pounded so I shook, down to my hardened aureole,

Its tiny halo enflamed, engorged with milk—
Where He hesitated only a millisecond before

Letting his finger meander further down, gravity
Lowering my eyes too, as slowly His fingertip undulated

Along the corrugation of my ribs, and down again,
Grazing now across my taut expanse of belly,

Where He paused momentarily to circle my navel softly
Before His finger moved on further down, down

To my tenderest mouth flushed with blood, blushing with
God's breath upon it, His finger rousing me there,

Stroking my trembling nether lips, rubbing them gently,
First the one, then the other, then the tiny tidal wave

That rose to meet His finger's playful, painful touch—
The aching, rising pitch of flesh turning everything to fire—

And then, all the universe—extinguished:
God took His hand away.

Notes on Desire

EVE ALEXANDRA

She tries to remember the origin of her desire. This child. This match. This tower. This tango. This sweat. This snare. This noose. This falling. This sleep. This voice in her head. *Scent.* Scent on her. This falling. This sweet. This weight. This crawling on her cunt. This arson. This mouth. This never-enough. She is afraid. To be in the same room with him. She is always. In the room with him. They are making the bed. Her lover's quilt. Heirloom. This room. This house they are building. This *home is where the heart is.* This never-enough. This constant. This voice. This *please go away.* This wife. This bitch. This bad girl. His shoulder. His red shirt. His work hands. His breath on her. They never suspect. In school she learns the names. For what's inside her. *There are five senses: sight,* s*ound, touch, taste, and smell. Scent.* Scent on her. She likes these five senses. In the first year. They made love. Now they fuck. She comes when *she* calls her *bitch, whore, my little slut.* She worries. Gets better and better. She doesn't want to ever go back. To love. To soft. She came into the world like this. A child with the knowledge of her own sexual power. She is wearing pink overalls. She is standing. Her chin resting on the rail. Her hands. Clutching the bars of her crib. Maybe that's why it happened. Maybe he smelled it on her. She was twenty-one. She said *Yes, yes.* It was summer. In trees. By the water. No moon. No stars. Just dark. The dark and their tongues. Their eyes. Their hands. Their scent. It's not always. Like this. Between women. Not always pretty like this. But just this once. It was dark. Hands. Tongues. Breasts. *Scent.* It was the first kiss. *I love you. Scent.* Scent on her. His breath. Work hands. His red shirt. *There are five senses.* She said *Yes,*

yes. She is this child. This match. She is this tango. This tower. This snare. She is this falling. This voice. Voice in her head. Falling. Sleep. *Scent.* Sweet. Heirloom. This room. This arson. This crawling on her cunt. She wears red. On the lips of her mouth. Bitch. Bad girl. Never-enough. It was the first kiss.

autopsky

KAI CHENG THOM

someday they'll cut this body open
and discover that my flesh is made of sky:
azure, sapphire, cerulean, turquoise, ultramarine
indigo
violet
black
cirrus and cumulus clouds stirring behind my eyes
cumulonimbus, alight with lightning,
crackling through the capillaries of the heart.
i am oh so full of rain
you could fall through me into forever.
please,
dear scientist, mortuary explorer, search me thoroughly
tenderly catalogue all my wayward parts.
find somewhere in me
the forgotten moon, the faded stars.
re-member, reassemble, this tattered heaven, this
shattered
celestial thing.

Untitled

GRACE PALEY

When this old body
finds that old body
what a nice day it is

when that old body
loves this old body
it's dreamless to sleep
and busy to wake up

when this old body says
you're a little lumpy here and there
but you're the same old body after all

old body   old body   in which somewhere
between crooked toe and forgetful head
the flesh encounters soul
and whispers   you

January Vineyards

RUTH L. SCHWARTZ

How our bodies fail to confine our longings,
even in death's season, withholding nothing

How the hills furrow like a cherished body,
leaning into the opened hand of the lake

How the brittle grapevines braid the fields

How the vagina clenches, prayerfully,
around the fingers which have entered it

How the canopy of leaves will bless the fruit,
each grape soft and ready for the mouth

> Sex was going to be the landscape
> which would make our bodies perfect,
> and it has

How savagely I want you, even here,
on the white stretcher, in the pallid hospital

There's Nothing More

WENDY VIDELOCK

There's nothing more
erotic than

one   red

Chilean plum
slumbered in

the brown palm
of the curved

hand of the right
man.

Acknowledgments

Sincerest thanks to Jessica Walen and Allyson Hoffman, both of whom provided help at critical junctures in the reading and editing processes. As ever, I am grateful to my agent, Rob McQuilken, and also to Robin Miura and Lynn York, the good women at Blair.

The editor and publisher gratefully aknowledge permisson to publish the following poems from the following organizations and individuals:

DIANE ACKERMAN, "Curtains of Goldenrod" and "Song of the Current at Cape Horn" from *Jaguar of Sweet Laughter: New and Selected Poems.* Copyright © 1993 by Diane Ackerman. Used by permission of Random House, an imprint and division of Penguin Random House LLC. All rights reserved.

"Searching for the Comet" from *I Praise My Destroyer.* Copyright © 2000 by Diane Ackerman. Used by permission of Random House, an imprint and division of Penguin Random House LLC. All rights reserved.

KIM ADDONIZIO, "'What Do Women Want?'" from *Tell Me.* Copyright © 2000 by Kim Addonizio. Reprinted with the permission of The Permissions Company, Inc., on behalf of BOA Editions, Ltd., www.boaeditions.org.

"First Poem for You" from *The Philosopher's Club* (Rochester, NY: BOA Editions, 1994). Copyright © 1994 by Kim Addonizio. Used by permission of the author.

Contributors

DIANE ACKERMAN

Diane Ackerman is the author of two dozen highly acclaimed works of poetry and nonfiction, including *New York Times* best sellers *The Zookeeper's Wife*, *A Natural History of the Senses*, *The Human Age*, and Pulitzer Prize Finalist, *One Hundred Names for Love*.

KIM ADDONIZIO

Kim Addonizio is the author of a dozen books, most recently *Bukowski in a Sundress: Confessions from a Writing Life* (Penguin), and the poetry collection *Mortal Trash* (W. W. Norton). Her work has appeared in the *New York Times*, *Poetry*, the *Sun*, and numerous literary journals and anthologies. She has received fellowships from the NEA and Guggenheim Foundations, two Pushcart Prizes, and other honors. She offers poetry workshops privately in Oakland, California, and online. www.kimaddonizio.com

ELIZABETH ALEXANDER

Elizabeth Alexander is a poet, essayist, playwright, and teacher. In 2009, she composed and delivered "Praise Song for the Day" for the inauguration of President Barack Obama. She has published six books of poems, two collections of essays, and a play. Her book of poems, *American Sublime* (2005), was one of three finalists for the Pulitzer Prize and was one of the American Library Association's "Notable Books of the Year." Her play, *Diva Studies* (1996), was produced at the Yale School of Drama. Her memoir, *The Light of the World*, was released to widespread acclaim in April 2015.

EVE ALEXANDRA

Eve Alexandra is the author of *The Drowned Girl* (Kent State University Press, 2003). She teaches at the University of Vermont.

NINA RUBINSTEIN ALONSO

Nina Rubinstein Alonso is the editor of *Constellations: A Journal of Poetry and Fiction* (constellations-lit.com) and has published in the *New Yorker*, *Ploughshares*, *Ibbetson Street*, *Sumac*, *New Boston Review*, *U. Mass. Review*, and other publications. Her book *This Body* was published by David Godine Press. She is also the director and head teacher of Fresh Pond Ballet School in Cambridge, Massachusetts.

IDRIS ANDERSON

Idris Anderson's second collection of poems *Doubtful Harbor* was selected by Sherod Santos for the Hollis Summers Prize and published by Ohio University Press (2018). Her first collection of poems *Mrs. Ramsay's Knee* was selected by Harold Bloom for the May Swenson Poetry Award and published by Utah State University Press. She has won a Pushcart Prize and the Yeats Society of New York Poetry Prize and has published poems in *AGNI*, *Crab Orchard Review*, the *Hudson Review*, *Michigan Quarterly Review*, *Paris Review*, *Plume*, *Southern Review*, and other journals. She was born and grew up in Charleston, South Carolina, and has lived in the San Francisco Bay Area for more than two decades.

MAYA ANGELOU

Maya Angelou (1928–2014) was raised in Stamps, Arkansas. In addition to her bestselling autobiographies, including *I Know Why the Caged Bird Sings* and *The Heart of a Woman*, she wrote numerous volumes of poetry, among them *Phenomenal Woman*, *And Still I Rise*, *On the Pulse of Morning*, and *Mother*.

COLETTE LABOUFF ATKINSON

Colette LaBouff Atkinson is the author of *Mean*, a collection of prose poems (University of Chicago Press, 2008). Her prose has been featured in the *Los Angeles Times*, *Seneca Review*, *Santa Monica Review*, *Orange Coast Magazine*, *Babble*, and elsewhere.

WENDY BARKER

Wendy Barker's sixth collection of poetry, winner of the John Ciardi Prize, is *One Blackbird at a Time* (BkMk Press, 2015). Her fourth chapbook of poems is *From the Moon, Earth Is Blue* (Wings Press, 2015). Other books include *Far Out: Poems of the '60s* (co-edited with Dave Parsons, Wings Press, 2016), *Poems' Progress* (Absey & Co., 2002), and a selection of co-translations, *Rabindranath Tagore: Final Poems* (Braziller, 2001). Her poems have appeared in numerous journals and anthologies, including *The Best American Poetry 2013*. Recipient of NEA and Rockefeller fellowships, she teaches at the University of Texas at San Antonio.

ELLEN BASS

Ellen Bass's most recent book is *Like a Beggar* (Copper Canyon Press, 2014). She co-edited the groundbreaking *No More Masks! An Anthology of Poems by Women* and her nonfiction books include *The Courage to Heal* and *Free Your Mind*. Her poetry frequently appears in the *New Yorker*, the *American Poetry Review*, and many other journals. Among her awards are fellowships from the National Endowment for the Arts and the California Arts Council, three Pushcart Prizes, and the Lambda Literary Award. A chancellor of the Academy of American Poets, she teaches in the MFA writing program at Pacific University. www.ellenbass.com

ROBIN BECKER

The Black Bear Inside Me, Robin Becker's sixth book in the Pitt Poetry Series, came out in 2018. She has received fellowships from the Massachusetts Cultural Council, the NEA, and the Radcliffe Institute for Advanced Study at Harvard. She regularly reviews poetry for the *Georgia Review* and served as poetry editor for the *Women's Review of Books*. Liberal Arts Research Professor Emeritus at Penn State, Becker's recent poems have appeared in the *American Poetry Review* and the *New Yorker*.

Erin Belieu is the author of four books of poetry: *Infanta* (1995), selected by Hayden Carruth for the National Poetry Series; *One Above, One Below* (2000); *Black Box* (2006), a finalist for the Los Angeles Times Book Prize; and *Slant Six* (2014). Belieu co-edited, with Susan Aizenberg, the anthology *The Extraordinary Tide: New Poetry by American Women* (2001). With poet Cate Marvin, Belieu cofounded and codirects VIDA: Women in the Literary Arts, an organization that seeks to "explore critical and cultural perceptions of writing by women" in contemporary culture.

JILL BIALOSKY

Jill Bialosky is the author of four acclaimed collections of poetry, most recently *The Players*. Her poems have appeared in the *New Yorker*, the *New York Times*, *Kenyon Review*, *Atlantic*, and *Best American Poetry*. She is the author of three novels, most recently *The Prize*, and two works of nonfiction, a *New York Times* bestselling memoir, *History of a Suicide: My Sister's Unfinished Life*, and *Poetry Will Save Your Life*. She was honored by the Poetry Society of America for her distinguished contribution to the field.

LAURA BOSS

Laura Boss is a first-place winner of Poetry Society of America's Gordon Barber Poetry Contest. Founder and editor of *Lips*, she was the sole representative of the USA at the XXVI Annual Struga International Poetry Readings in Macedonia. Her awards for her poetry also include three poetry fellowships from the New Jersey State Council on the Arts. Boss's seven books of poetry include *Arms: New and Selected Poems* (Guernica Editions) and most recently, *The Best Lover* (NYQ). In 2011 she received the first International Poetry Award at the International Poetry Festival in Swansea, Wales. Her poems have appeared in the *New York Times*.

OLGA BROUMAS

Olga Broumas was born on Syros, a Cycladic island, in Greece. She received a Fulbright fellowship in 1967 and immigrated to the

United States. Broumas earned her BA from the University of Pennsylvania and MFA from the University of Oregon. Her first book to appear in the United States, *Beginning with O* (1977), won the Yale Younger Poets Award. Her work, which has been described as "Sapphic," attempts to create a language attentive to Eros and Justice. Her many collections of poetry include *Soie Sauvage* (1979), *Pastoral Jazz* (1983), *Perpetua* (1989), and *Rave: Poems 1975–1999* (1999). Her most recent is *Sappho's Gymnasium* (2017), co-authored with T Begley (Nightboat).

JAYNE RELAFORD BROWN

Jayne Relaford Brown is the author of *My First Real Tree*, a poetry volume published by FootHill Publishing. Her poem "Finding Her Here," ("I am becoming the woman I've wanted") has been widely reprinted and made into a poster and a choral work for women's voices. She is a recently retired creative writing and composition teacher who lives with her partner of thirty years near Kutztown, Pennsylvania.

STEPHANIE BURT

Stephanie Burt is a professor of English at Harvard. She is the author of several books of poetry and literary criticism, most recently *Advice from the Lights* (Graywolf, 2017); her essays and reviews appear in the *New York Times Book Review*, the *London Review of Books*, *Rain Taxi*, and other journals in the UK, the US, and New Zealand.

STACIE CASSARINO

Stacie Cassarino earned a BA from Middlebury College in Vermont and an MA from the University of Washington. Her poems have appeared in the *New Republic*, the *Iowa Review*, *AGNI*, the *Georgia Review*, *Indiana Review*, and other journals. Her first collection of poetry is *Zero at the Bone* (2009). Cassarino received the 2007 Astraea Lesbian Writers Fund Award in Poetry and the "Discovery"/ *The Nation* Joan Leiman Jacobsen Poetry Prize in 2005. She has been nominated for the Rona Jaffe Writers' Award and twice for the Pushcart Prize. *Zero at the Bone* was nominated for a Lambda Literary Award in Poetry.

LORNA DEE CERVANTES

Lorna Dee Cervantes is an internationally acclaimed Chicana poet from San José, California. Her first book, *Emplumada* (University of Pittsburgh Press, 1981) won an American Book Award; her second, *From the Cables of Genocide: Poems on Love and Hunger* (Arte Público Press, 1991) won the Paterson Prize for Best Book of Poetry and the Latino Literature Award. Her next book *DRIVE: The First Quartet* (2006) received the International Latino Book Award. Her most recent book is *Ciento: 100 100-Word Love Poems*.

JENNIFER CHANG

Jennifer Chang is the author of *The History of Anonymity*, which was a finalist for the Glasgow/Shenandoah Prize for Emerging Writers and listed by *Hyphen* magazine as a Top Five Book of Poetry for 2008. Her poems have appeared in *American Poetry Review*, *Best American Poetry 2012*, the *Nation*, *Poetry*, *A Public Space*, and elsewhere. She is an assistant professor of English and creative writing at George Washington University and lives in Washington, DC, with her family.

MAXINE CHERNOFF

Maxine Chernoff is the author of twenty-two books, six in fiction and sixteen in poetry. She is a winner of a 2013 NEA fellowship in poetry, the 2009 PEN Translation Award, and was a 2016 Visiting Writer at the American Academy in Rome. She is professor and former chair of the Creative Writing Department at San Francisco State University and former editor of *New American Writing*.

CHRYSTOS

Chrystos is a poet and activist and author of a novel and five poetry collections, including *Fugitive Colors* (Cleveland State University Poetry Center, 1995), *Firepower* (Press Gang, 1995), and *In Her I Am* (Press Gang, 1993). Chrystos has been the recipient of an NEA Arts Fellowship, a Lannan Foundation Grant, the Audre Lord International Poetry Award, a Sappho Award, a Barbara Deming Memorial Grant, and the Fund for Human Rights Freedom of Expression Award.

SANDRA CISNEROS

Sandra Cisneros is an activist poet, short story writer, novelist, essayist, and artist. Her numerous awards include NEA fellowships in both poetry and prose, the Texas Medal of the Arts, a MacArthur Fellowship, several honorary degrees, and both national and international book awards. Most recently, she received the Ford Foundation's Art of Change Fellowship, Chicago's Fifth Star Award, the PEN Center USA Literary Award, the Arthur R. Velasquez Award from the National Museum of Mexican Art in Chicago and Loyola University's Arts and Science Damen Award, presented to Loyola alumni in recognition of their leadership in industry, the community, and service to others.

CHERYL CLARKE

Poet and essayist Cheryl Clarke has written many books, including *Narratives: poems in the tradition of black women* (1982), *Living as a Lesbian* (1986), *Humid Pitch* (1989), *Experimental Love* (1993), the critical study, *After Mecca: Women Poets and the Black Arts Movement* (Rutgers University Press, 2005), and *The Days of Good Looks: Prose and Poetry 1980–2005* (Carroll and Graf, 2006). Her latest manuscript, "By My Precise Haircut," was selected as one of two winners of the Hilary Tham Capital Competition, sponsored by the Word Works Press of Washington, DC, and judged by poet Kimiko Hahn.

LUCILLE CLIFTON

Lucille Clifton (1936–2010) won the Ruth Lilly Poetry Prize in 2007, a National Book Award in 2000, was two-time finalist for a Pulitzer Prize, and served as the poet laureate of Maryland from 1974–1985. In addition to her many collections of poetry, including *Good Woman: Poems and a Memoir: 1969–1980*, *Next: New Poems*, and *Blessing the Boats: New and Collected Poems 1988–2000*, she also wrote many children's books, among them *The Boy Who Didn't Believe in Spring* and *The Lucky Stone*.

CAROLYN CREEDON

Carolyn Creedon is a writer, editor, and fifteen-year veteran of the waitress wars. She completed the Ada Comstock program at Smith College, went on to earn an MA, then to the University of Virginia where she earned an MFA and was the recipient of the Academy of American Poets Prize. Her poems have been published in the *Massachusetts Review*, *Best New Poets*, *Best of the Best American Poets*, *Ploughshares*, *Yale Review*, *Rattle*, the *American Poetry Review*, and other journals. In 2010 she won the Alehouse Happy Hour Poetry Prize. She lives in Charlottesville, Virginia, with her husband and her dog.

ALISON HAWTHORNE DEMING

Alison Hawthorne Deming's most recent books are the poetry collection *Stairway to Heaven*, the essay collection *Zoologies: On Animals and the Human Spirit*, and *Death Valley: Painted Light*, a collaboration with photographer Stephen Strom. A recent Guggenheim Fellow, she is the author of three additional nonfiction books and four previous poetry books, including *Science and Other Poems*, which won the Walt Whitman Award. She is Agnese Nelms Haury Chair in Environment and Social Justice and Regents' Professor at the University of Arizona.

DIANE DI PRIMA

Diane di Prima is the author of more than forty books, including poetry collections *The Poetry Deal* (City Lights Publishers, 2014), *Pieces of a Song: Selected Poems* (City Lights Publishers, 1990), and *This Kind of Bird Flies Backwards* (Totem Press, 1958), as well as nonfiction, novels, short stories, and plays. She is the recipient of two grants from the National Endowment for the Arts.

MOIRA EGAN

A resident of Rome, Italy, Moira Egan earned a BA from Bryn Mawr College, an MA from the Johns Hopkins University Writing Seminars, and an MFA from Columbia University, where James Merrill chose her graduate manuscript for the David Craig Austin Prize. Her most recent collection, *Synæsthesium* (2017), won the New Criterion Poetry Prize. Previous books published in the US are *Hot Flash Sonnets* (2013); *Spin* (2010); *Bar Napkin Sonnets* (2009), which won the 2008 Ledge Poetry Chapbook Competition; and *Cleave* (2004).

KATHLEEN FLENNIKEN

Kathleen Flenniken is the author of two poetry collections, *Famous* (University of Nebraska Press, 2006), named a Notable Book by the American Library Association, and *Plume* (University of Washington Press, 2012), a finalist for the William Carlos Williams Award. Her other awards include fellowships from the NEA and Artist Trust, a Pushcart Prize, the Prairie Schooner Book Prize for Poetry, and the Washington State Book Award. She served as Washington State Poet Laureate from 2012–2014.

ALICE FRIMAN

Alice Friman's seventh collection, *Blood Weather*, is forthcoming from Louisiana State University Press. Her last two books are *The View from Saturn* and *Vinculum*, for which she won the 2012 Georgia Author of the Year Award in Poetry. Other books include *Inverted Fire* and *The Book of the Rotten Daughter,* both from BkMk, and *Zoo,* from University of Arkansas Press, which won the Sheila Margaret Motton Prize from New England Poetry Club and the Ezra Pound Poetry Award from Truman State University. She is a recipient of a Pushcart Prize, is included in *Best American Poetry,* and is the winner of the 2016 Paumanok Award. Professor emerita of English and creative writing at the University of Indianapolis, she lives in Milledgeville, Georgia, where she was poet-in-residence at Georgia College.

JANE ANN (DEVOL) FULLER

Jane Ann (Devol) Fuller is a graduate of the Iowa Writers' Workshop. In 2000, she co-authored *Revenants: A Story of Many Lives*, published with a grant from the Ohio Arts Council. Her poetry also appears in *Aethlon: Journal of Sport Literature*, *Atticus Review*, *Fifth Wednesday*, the *Pikeville Review*, *Pudding Magazine*, *Waccamaw*, *jmww*, *Steinbeck Now*, and in the anthology *Project Hope* published by the Center for Victims of Torture. Local collaboratives include *Women on the Line* and *Women of Appalachia Project*. In 2015, Jane Ann was awarded the James Boatwright III Poetry Prize for a poem about baseball and learning to fiddle.

ALICE FULTON

Alice Fulton is the recipient of an American Academy of Arts and Letters Award in Literature and has also received fellowships in poetry from the John D. and Catherine T. MacArthur Foundation, the Ingram Merrill Foundation, the Guggenheim Foundation, the Michigan Society of Fellows, the Fine Arts Work Center in Provincetown, and the National Endowment for the Arts. Her book *Felt* was awarded the Rebekah Johnson Bobbitt National Prize for Poetry from the Library of Congress. Other books include *Barely Composed*; *Sensual Math*; *Powers of Congress*; *Palladium*, winner of the National Poetry Series and the Society of Midland Authors Award; and *Dance Script With Electric Ballerina*, winner of the Associated Writing Programs Award.

ELIZABETH W. GARBER

Elizabeth W. Garber is the author of *Implosion: A Memoir of an Architect's Daughter* (2018); three books of poetry, *True Affections* (2012), *Listening Inside the Dance* (2005), and *Pierced by the Seasons* (2004); and *Maine (Island Time)* (2013), a collaboration of her poetry with paintings and photographs of Michael Weymouth. Three of her poems have been read on NPR's *The Writer's Almanac*. She was awarded writing fellowships at the Virginia Center for Creative Arts and the Jentel Artist Residency Program in Wyoming. She has maintained a private practice as an acupuncturist for more than thirty years in mid-coast Maine, where she raised her family. www .elizabethgarber.com

AMY GERSTLER

Amy Gerstler received her BA in psychology from Pitzer College in 1978 and her MFA in nonfiction from Bennington College in 2000. Her books of poetry include *Scattered at Sea* (Penguin, 2015), which was longlisted for the 2015 National Book Award; *Dearest Creature* (Penguin, 2009); and *Medicine* (Penguin, 2000), which was a finalist for the Phi Beta Kappa Poetry Award. Gerstler is the author of art reviews, books reviews, fiction, and various journal articles. Gerstler has taught at Antioch University and the University of California at Irvine. She currently teaches in the Bennington Writing Seminars program at Bennington College and at Art Center College of Design in Pasadena, California. She lives in Los Angeles, California.

NIKKI GIOVANNI

Poet Nikki Giovanni was born in Knoxville, Tennessee, on June 7, 1943. Although she grew up in Cincinnati, Ohio, she and her sister returned to Knoxville each summer to visit their grandparents. Nikki graduated with honors in history from her grandfather's alma mater, Fisk University. She has been awarded an unprecedented seven NAACP Image Awards. She has been nominated for a Grammy and been a finalist for the National Book Award. She has authored three *New York Time*s and *Los Angeles Times* best sellers. Since 1987, she has been on the faculty at Virginia Tech, where she is a University Distinguished Professor.

LOUISE GLÜCK

Louise Glück is the author of numerous books of poetry, most recently, *Faithful and Virtuous Night* (Farrar, Straus, and Giroux, 2014), which won the 2014 National Book Award in Poetry; *Poems 1962–2012* (Farrar, Straus, and Giroux, 2012); *A Village Life: Poems* (Farrar, Straus, and Giroux, 2009); *Averno* (Farrar, Straus, and Giroux, 2006), a finalist for the 2006 National Book Award in Poetry; *The Seven Ages* (Ecco Press, 2001); and *Vita Nova* (Ecco Press, 1999), winner of *Boston Book Review*'s Bingham Poetry Prize and the *New Yorker*'s Book Award in Poetry.

BARBARA GOLDBERG

Barbara Goldberg authored five prize-winning books of poetry, including *The Royal Baker's Daughter*, winner of the Felix Pollak Poetry Prize. Her most recent book is *The Kingdom of Speculation*, with *Transformations: The Poetry of Translation* forthcoming. Goldberg received two fellowships from the National Endowment for the Arts as well as awards from Columbia University's Translation Center and PEN's Syndicated Fiction Project. Her work appears in *Best American Poetry*, *Paris Review*, *Poetry*, the *Gettysburg Review*, and elsewhere. She is series editor for the International Editions at The Word Works. Goldberg lives in Chevy Chase, Maryland.

ANGELINA WELD GRIMKÉ

Angelina Weld Grimké (1880–1958) was a playwright, poet, author, and teacher during the Harlem Renaissance. She was one of the first African-American women to have one of her plays publicly performed.

BETH GYLYS

A professor of creative writing at Georgia State University, Beth Gylys has published three books of poetry, *Sky Blue Enough to Drink* (Grayson Books, 2016), *Spot in the Dark* (The Journal Award, Ohio State University Press, 2005), and *Bodies that Hum* (Gerald Cable First Book Award, Silverfish Review Press, 1999), and two chapbooks *Matchbook* (La Vita Poetica Press, 2007) and *Balloon Heart* (Quentin R. Howard Competition, Wind Press, 1997). Her work has appeared in *Rattle*, *Barrow Street*, *Southern Review*, *New Republic*, *Paris Review*, and many other journals and anthologies.

BRENDA HILLMAN

Brenda Hillman (b. 1951) is a poet, educator, editor, and activist; she is the author of ten collections of poetry with Wesleyan University Press, most recently *Seasonal Works with Letters on Fire* (2013), and *Extra Hidden Life, Among the Days*, (2018). She has also cotranslated *At Your Feet* by Ana Cristina Cesar (Parlor Press/Free Verse Editions, 2018). Hillman serves as the Filippi Professor of Poetry at Saint Mary's College of California.

JANE HIRSHFIELD
Jane Hirshfield's eighth poetry book is *The Beauty*, long-listed for the 2015 National Book Award. She is also the author of two books of essays, *Nine Gates* and *Ten Windows*, and editor/co-translator of four books collecting world poets from the past. Honors include fellowships from the Guggenheim and Rockefeller foundations, NEA, Academy of American Poets, and the Poetry Center and California Book Awards. A chancellor emerita of The Academy of American Poets, Hirshfield's work appears in the *New Yorker*, the *Atlantic*, the *New Republic*, *Harper's*, the *Paris Review*, *Poetry*, and eight editions of *The Best American Poetry*.

MARIE HOWE
Marie Howe is the author of four volumes of poetry: *Magdalene: Poems* (W. W. Norton, 2017); *The Kingdom of Ordinary Time* (W. W. Norton, 2009); *What the Living Do* (1997); and *The Good Thief* (1988). She is also the co-editor of a book of essays, *In the Company of My Solitude: American Writing from the AIDS Pandemic* (1994). Her poems have appeared in the *New Yorker*, the *Atlantic, Poetry*, *Agni, Ploughshares, Harvard Review*, and the *Partisan Review*, among others.

ERICA JONG
Fear of Flying, Erica Jong's first and most famous novel published in 1973, blew conventional thinking about women, marriage, and sexuality out of the water, selling over 37 million copies and being translated into over 45 languages including Chinese and Arabic. Comfortable and eloquent in various genres, she has switched between fiction, nonfiction, and poetry almost effortlessly, becoming one of the most evocative poets of her generation with seven published volumes, and winning *Poetry* magazine's Bess Hokin Prize. Erica has won many awards for poetry and fiction all over the world. These

awards include: the Fernanda Pivano Award in Italy, the Sigmund Freud Award in Italy, the Deauville Award in France, and the United Nations Award for excellence in literature.

LENORE KANDEL

Lenore Kandel (1932–2009) was born in New York City and wrote poetry from childhood. The author of *The Love Book* (1966) and *Word Alchemy* (1967), she died at the age of 77.

MAXINE KUMIN

Maxine Kumin (1925–2014) published numerous books of poetry, including *And Short the Season: Poems* (W. W. Norton, 2014); *Where I Live: New & Selected Poems 1990–2010* (W. W. Norton, 2010); *Still to Mow* (2009); *Jack* (2003); *The Long Marriage* (2003); *Bringing Together* (2003); *Connecting the Dots* (1996); *Looking for Luck* (1992), which received the Poets' Prize; *Nurture* (1989); *The Long Approach* (1986); *Our Ground Time Here Will Be Brief* (1982); *House, Bridge, Fountain, Gate* (1975); and *Up Country: Poems of New England* (1972), for which she received the Pulitzer Prize.

DORIANNE LAUX

Dorianne Laux's award-winning books, *Facts About the Moon* and *The Book of Men*, are available from W. W. Norton. Her poems have been translated into French, Italian, Spanish, Korean, Romanian, Dutch, Afrikkans, and Brazilian Portuguese. Her "New and Selected" collection, *Only as the Day Is Long*, is forthcoming in January 2019 from W. W. Norton. She teaches poetry at North Carolina State University and is founding faculty at Pacific University's Low Residency MFA Program.

WENDY LEE

Wendy Lee is the poetry pen name for Wendy Maltz, an author, therapist, and national expert in the area of sexual health and healing. Wendy compiled and edited two highly acclaimed poetry anthologies—*Passionate Hearts: The Poetry of Sexual Love* and *Intimate*

Kisses: The Poetry of Sexual Pleasure. Her other books include *The Sexual Healing Journey*, *Private Thoughts*, and *The Porn Trap*. Her website is www.healthySex.com. Wendy believes sexual love poetry is the most soul-stirring way to convey the universal beauty and pleasures of sex.

DENISE LEVERTOV

Denise Levertov (1923–1997) is the author of more than thirty books, including *Making Peace*, *Sands of the Well*, and *The Stream and the Sapphire*. Along with the Elmer Holmes Bobst Award in poetry and the Lannan Prize, she won the 1996 Governor's Writers Award from the Washington State Commission for the Humanities.

ADA LIMÓN

Ada Limón is the author of five books of poetry, including *Bright Dead Things*, which was named a finalist for the 2015 National Book Award in Poetry, a finalist for the Kingsley Tufts Poetry Award, a finalist for the 2016 National Book Critics Circle Award, and one of the Top Ten Poetry Books of the Year by the *New York Times*. Her other books include *Lucky Wreck*, *This Big Fake World*, and *Sharks in the Rivers*. She serves on the faculty of Queens University of Charlotte Low Residency MFA program, and the 24PearlStreet online program for the Provincetown Fine Arts Work Center.

AUDRE LORDE

The Black feminist, lesbian, poet, mother, warrior Audre Lorde (1934–1992) was a native New Yorker and daughter of immigrants. Both her activism and her published work speak to the importance of struggle for liberation among oppressed peoples and of organizing in coalition across differences of race, gender, sexual orientation, class, age, and ability. An internationally recognized activist and artist, Audre Lorde was the recipient of many honors and awards, including the Walt Whitman Citation of Merit, which conferred the mantle of New York State poet for 1991–1993.

BARBARA O'DAIR

Barbara O'Dair is an editor and writer who lives in New Jersey.

SHARON OLDS

Sharon Olds's first collection of poems, *Satan Says* (University of Pittsburgh Press, 1980), received the inaugural San Francisco Poetry Center Award. Olds's following collection, *The Dead & the Living* (Alfred A. Knopf, 1984), received the Lamont Poetry Selection in 1983 and the National Book Critics Circle Award. She has written many other collections, including *Stag's Leap* (Alfred A. Knopf, 2012), recipient of the Pulitzer Prize and the T. S. Eliot Prize; *One Secret Thing* (Random House, 2008); and *The Father* (Alfred A. Knopf, 1992); which was shortlisted for the T. S. Eliot Prize and was a finalist for the National Book Critics Circle Award.

GRACE PALEY

Grace Paley (1922–2007) published many books of fiction and poetry, including *Later the Same Day* (1985), *Leaning Forward* (1985), and *The Collected Stories* (1994), which was a finalist for both the Pulitzer Prize and National Book Award. In 1961, Paley was awarded a Guggenheim Fellowship. In 1989, she was deemed the first official New York State Writer by New York governor Mario Cuomo. Other honors include a National Endowment for the Arts fellowship in 1967, the Edith Wharton Award in 1983, and the Jewish Cultural Achievement Award in the Literary Arts in 1994. She was Vermont State Poet Laureate (2003–2007).

MOLLY PEACOCK

Molly Peacock is a widely anthologized poet who began writing erotic poems from a woman's point of view because she couldn't find enough of them to read. Her seventh collection is *The Analyst* (W. W. Norton), poems that tell the story of a decades-long patient-therapist relationship that reverses and continues to evolve after the analyst's stroke. Peacock is also a noted biographer and memoirist. Passionate about bringing poetry to a wider public, she helped inaugurate Poetry in Motion on New York City's subways and buses. Sensuous poems by women on subway car posters? Not yet . . .

MARGE PIERCY

Marge Piercy has written seventeen novels, including the *New York Times* best seller *Gone to Soldiers*; the National Bestsellers *Braided Lives* and *The Longings of Women*; the classics *Woman on the Edge of Time* and *He, She and It*; and most recently *Sex Wars*. Among her nineteen volumes of poetry the most recently published include *The Hunger Moon: New & Selected Poems 1980–2010* and *Made in Detroit*. Her critically acclaimed memoir is *Sleeping with Cats*. Born in center city Detroit, educated at the University of Michigan and Northwestern, the recipient of four honorary doctorates, she is active in antiwar, feminist, and environmental causes.

DEIDRE POPE

Deidre Pope has published in the *Beloit Poetry Journal*, *Northwest Review*, *Tar River Poetry*, and *Spoon River Poetry Review*, among others, and the anthologies *What's Become of Eden: Poems of Family at Century's End* and *My Lover Is a Woman: Contemporary Lesbian Love Poems*. She has received a Pushcart nomination and an MFA in poetry from Cornell University. She was a finalist in the New Issues Poetry Series for first poetry collections and her chapbook manuscript has twice been a finalist in national competitions. In 1999, she received a Minnesota State Arts Board Fellowship for poetry.

ADRIENNE RICH

Adrienne Rich (1929–2012) was born in Baltimore, Maryland. Over her long career, she published more than sixteen volumes of poetry and five volumes of critical prose, most recently *Tonight No Poetry Will Serve: Poems 2007–2010*, *A Human Eye: Essays on Art in Society*, and *Collected Poems: 1950–2012*, published posthumously. She edited Muriel Rukeyser's *Selected Poems* for the Library of America. Among numerous other recognitions, Rich was the 2006 recipient of the National Book Foundation's Medal for Distinguished Contribution to

American Letters. Her poetry and essays have been widely translated and published internationally.

KATHERINE RIEGEL

Katherine Riegel is the author of *Letters to Colin Firth*, which won the 2015 Sundress Publications Chapbook Competition, and two books of poetry: *What the Mouth Was Made For* and *Castaway*. Her poems and essays have appeared in *Brevity, The Offing, Orion, Poets.org, Tin House*, and elsewhere. She is cofounder and poetry editor for *Sweet: A Literary Confection*.

PATTIANN ROGERS

Pattiann Rogers is the recipient of two NEA grants, a Guggenheim Fellowship, and a Lannan Poetry Fellowship. Her numerous books of poetry include *Holy Heathen Rhapsody* (Penguin, 2013), *Wayfare* (Penguin, 2008), *Generations* (Penguin, 2004), and *Song of the World Becoming: New and Collected Poems, 1981–2001* (Milkweed Editions, 2001).

JUNE SYLVESTER SARACENO

June Sylvester Saraceno is the author of two poetry collections, *Of Dirt and Tar*, and *Altars of Ordinary Light*, as well as a chapbook of prose poems, *Mean Girl Trips*. Her work has appeared in various journals, including *Blue Lyra Review, Southwestern American Literature*, and *Tar River Poetry*. She is English program chair at Sierra Nevada College, Lake Tahoe, as well as MFA faculty and founding editor of the *Sierra Nevada Review*. For more information visit www .junesaraceno.com.

RUTH L. SCHWARTZ

Ruth L. Schwartz's five books of poems include the National Poetry Series winner *Edgewater* (HarperCollins, 2002), selected by Jane Hirshfield. Her other poetry books are *Miraculum* (Autumn House Press, 2012), *Dear Good Naked Morning* (Autumn House Press, 2005), *Singular Bodies* (Anhinga Press, 2001), and *Accordion Breathing & Dancing* (University of Pittsburgh Press, 1996). Ruth has been the recipient of fellowships from the National Endowment for the Arts, the Ohio Arts Council, the Astraea Foundation, and the Henry Hoyns scholarship at the University of Michigan.

ANNE SEXTON

Anne Sexton (1928–1974) won the Pulitzer Prize for poetry in 1967 for her collection *Live or Die*. She received numerous prizes, awards, and honors, including a Guggenheim Fellowship, the Radcliffe Institute Fellowship, and the Levinson Prize.

ENID SHOMER

Enid Shomer is the author of eight books of poetry and prose, including *The Twelve Rooms of the Nile* (Simon & Schuster), which National Public Radio named one of the best novels of the year. Her work has appeared in the *New Yorker*, *Poetry*, the *Atlantic*, the *Paris Review*, and other publications. She won the Iowa Fiction Prize for her story collection *Imaginary Men* and the Florida Gold Medal in Fiction for *Tourist Season: Stories*. She has twice received fellowships in poetry from the National Endowment for the Arts. Longtime editor of the University of Arkansas Press Poetry Series, she received the Lifetime Achievement Award in Writing from the Florida Humanities Council.

MAURYA SIMON

Maurya Simon currently serves as a professor of the Graduate Division and a professor emerita at the University of California at Riverside. She is the author of ten volumes of poetry, including *The Wilderness, New & Selected Poems* (Red Hen Press, 2018). Additional books include: *Speaking in Tongues*, a nominee for the 1990 Pulitzer Prize, and *Ghost Orchid*, which was nominated in 2004 for a National Book Award in Poetry. Simon has been the recipient of a Poetry Fellowship from the National Endowment for the Arts, as well as a University Award from the Academy of American Poets, the Celia B. Wagner and Lucille Medwick Memorial Awards from the Poetry Society of America, and a 1991 Fulbright/Indo-American Fellowship.

DEBRA SPENCER

Debra Spencer invented her own alphabet when she was three. She wrote her first book in the second grade and went on to earn a BA from the University of California at Santa Cruz in 1972 and an MA from San Jose State University in 1988, where she won the Anne Lillis Memorial Scholarship for Poetry. In her desk she keeps a Bart Giammati baseball card, a fossilized shark's tooth, the tuning key to an Anglian harp, and a piece of the Berlin Wall.

SHERYL ST. GERMAIN

A native of New Orleans, Sheryl St. Germain is of Cajun and Creole descent. Her awards include two NEA Fellowships, an NEH Fellowship, the Dobie-Paisano Fellowship, and the William Faulkner award for the personal essay. Her poetry books include *Going Home*, *The Mask of Medusa*, *Making Bread at Midnight*, *How Heavy the Breath of God*, and *The Journals of Scheherazade*. She has also published a book of translations of the Cajun poet Jean Arceneaux, *Je Suis Cadien*. *Swamp Songs: The Making of an Unruly Woman*, a collection of essays about growing up in New Orleans, was published in 2003. She currently directs the MFA Creative Writing Program at Chatham University in Pittsburgh, where she teaches poetry and creative nonfiction. She has one son, Gray Gideon, who lives in Texas.

KAI CHENG THOM

Kai Cheng Thom, aka Lady Sin Trayda, is a fiery writer, performer, spoken word artist, and drag-dance sensation. Her first novel, *Fierce Femmes and Notorious Liars: A Dangerous Trans Girl's Confabulous Memoir* was recently published by Metonymy Press, and her first full-length poetry collection *a place called No Homeland* was published by Arsenal Pulp Press in April 2017. Kai Cheng has been widely published as an essayist and poet. Her poetry has appeared in *Matrix Magazine, ditch, OutWrite: A Queer Review*, and *What If? Magazine*, as well as the anthology *Where the Nights Are Twice as Long: Love Letters of Canadian Poets*.

WENDY VIDELOCK

Wendy Videlock lives on the Western Slope of the Colorado Rockies. Her first full-length collection, *Nevertheless*, came out in 2011 and was a finalist for the 2012 Colorado Book Award, followed by *The Dark Gnu* in 2013, a book she illustrated. Her chapbook, *What's That Supposed to Mean*, appeared in 2009. Her poems have been published widely in literary journals, most notably in *Poetry* and the *New York Times*.

TERRY WOLVERTON

Terry Wolverton is the author of eleven books of poetry, fiction, and creative nonfiction, including *Embers*, a novel in poems, and *Insurgent Muse: Life and Art at the Woman's Building.* She is the founder of Writers at Work, a creative writing studio in Los Angeles, and affiliate faculty in the MFA Writers Program at Antioch University Los Angeles. http://terrywolverton.com